*Organization
Development
in Transition*

Organization Development in Transition

Evidence of an evolving profession

A. J. McLean
D. B. P. Sims
I. L. Mangham
D. Tuffield
University of Bath

1807 1982

175 YEARS OF PUBLISHING

JOHN WILEY & SONS

Chichester · New York · Brisbane · Toronto · Singapore

Library of Congress Cataloging in Publication Data:
Main entry under title:

Organization development in transition.

  Bibliography: p.
  Includes index.
  Contents: The methodological framework of the research — Consultant roles in organizational change — A micropolitical perspective — The genesis of interventions — [etc.]
  1. Organizational change.   I. McLean, A . J. (Adrian J.)
HD58.8.O727   658.4'06   81-16061

ISBN 0 471 10142 7   AACR2

British Library Cataloguing in Publication Data:

Organization development in transition.
  1. Organizational change
  I. McLean, A. J.
  658.4'06   HD58.8

ISBN 0 471 10142 7

Phototypeset by Dobbie Typesetting Service, Plymouth, Devon, England
Printed in Great Britain by The Pitman Press, Bath, Avon

Contents

Preface vii

1   Introduction   1

2   The Methodological Framework of the Research   9

3   Consultant Roles in Organizational Change..................... 21

4   A Micropolitical Perspective 43

5   The Genesis of Interventions 61

6   Planned Change: A Notion of Convenience..................... 84

7   Centred and Unintegrated Practitioners:
    A Continuum of Consulting Styles 97

8   Conclusion Emerging Themes 121

Index 129

Preface

We wish to thank the following people:

Joan Budge, for her eternal patience and hard work in typing and retyping the book in various drafts.

Paul Tosey, for providing invaluable assistance as sub-editor together with general encouragement and constructive criticism throughout.

Sally Hyder, for all the work she happily undertook as research officer.

The Officers of the Chemical and Allied Product Industry Training Board Research Sub-Committee, for funding the research, especially Pat Terry and John Russell.

Gillian Spriggs, for typing the final manuscript.

Those people who acted as subjects for our research, many of whom went to considerable lengths to provide us with information about their activities, and to comment on our findings.

Chapter 1

Introduction

This book is a presentation of some research findings. The research, entitled *Implications of Interventions in Organizations* (1980), was conducted between 1975 and 1979 by the authors and Sally Hyder, who was the full time research officer, from the Centre for the Study of Organizational Change and Development.

Like the research it describes, the book is about many things; client consultant relationships, research methods, organizational change, power, and politics. Our primary intentions in the research, however, were twofold. Firstly we wished to capture and record the activities of people professionally concerned with managing change in organizations and the reasons underlying their actions. In so doing it was our intention to compare our findings with that body of literature termed Organization Development (OD), both to re-evaluate some of the ideas, theories, prescriptions, and values to be found there, and perhaps to acknowledge the evolution of the subject some ten to fifteen years after it emerged as a distinctive entity.

Our second main intention was to make a contribution towards redressing a discrepancy that has been remarked upon with some regularity among writers on organizational change, namely the discrepancy between theoretical descriptions of interventions as contained in case studies and OD texts, and the 'reality' of OD as it is practised. Our purpose throughout the research was to assemble a body of detailed, first hand accounts from people centrally concerned with organizational change, and to identify patterns and themes within and between such accounts. Our overall aim was inductively to derive concepts relating to organizational change from what those involved said had happened. We wanted to counterbalance what we regarded as the predominantly prescriptive stances taken by many OD writers who seemed to be interested mainly in *post hoc* rationalizations of their own actions.

We believe that such descriptions of change projects as do exist are of limited usefulness in terms of the extent to which they further our understanding of how to facilitate change and of the change process generally. Usually they are written up after the event by some of the central actors in the case, or by people who would like to consider themselves as being central to events, and who naturally have a strong interest in presenting both themselves and their interventions in as favourable a light as possible. Such people have either academic or professional (or both) reputations to safeguard, and perhaps enhance. Furthermore, we believe that in rendering their accounts acceptable to the broader OD community, they present them using existing terms and constructs and construe their activities so as to imply that their actions were in accordance with existing and accepted theory. A major reason for undertaking this research lay in our dissatisfaction with such accounts. They seemed to us to be too plausible, too tidy, and the decisions were presented as being far more straightforward and uncomplicated than we had found them to be in our own experience. Such cases contained little sense of the confusion and uncertainty that we had encountered during supposedly similar exercises. Furthermore the terms and concepts that were involved by way of commentary and description of the case did not always seem appropriate in view of the more general exposition of the course of events contained in the body of the account, and in some cases actually contradicted the actions as described. A further mismatch was between such accounts of consultant interventions and the theory and practice of intervening as described in OD texts. Some cases portray certain aspects of an intervention as illustrating particular OD techniques or approaches while other features of the same intervention patently contravene major OD principles. Moreover the reasoning underlying key decisions taken by consultants is often left un-stated or glossed over. In short, the issue of 'why we chose to do this and not that', crucial as we see it to sharing understanding and developing theory, is rarely answered satisfactorily and in some instances is not even addressed.

A Case Example: Crisis Intervention in a Municipal Agency

We have chosen to illustrate our misgivings about written case studies of change by examining an account by Goodstein and Boyer (1972) of their intervention into a municipal organization in crisis. Before so doing, however, an explanation of our reasons for choosing this particular example is called for. In the early conversations between the researchers about our general sense of dissatisfaction with written case studies of change we decided to examine some such studies in close detail. This particular case was the first that we looked at. Probably because it confirmed our suspicions in a way that was, to us, glaringly apparent, and perhaps as a consequence of being the first that we had examined so closely, it provided a major stimulus to our research ambition and became something of a landmark in our thinking. We have not chosen it because we regard it as exception in any sense, but rather because it epitomizes for us the approach and style of many case studies.

Early in their account the authors emphasize the importance that they place on 'promoting open and honest communication within the department', and explicitly comment on openness as a value: 'The consultant's values are to support open communication and dialogue among those persons who are vitally concerned with the issues being addressed'. They describe drawing up a contract with the governing Board of Health to 'conduct interviews and group conferences with members of the Department and certain others related to the Department and its functions, and to develop action plans', as they considered appropriate in their professional judgement for the resolution of the current organization problems. They further agree a date by which a written report of their findings will be submitted to the Board.

When under pressure from the press for a 'complete and open sharing' of developments, and despite their assertion that the community generally have a vital concern in the issue, they decline on the grounds that they feel that the time is 'premature and inappropriate'. The consultants, we learn, are the arbiters of appropriateness, but they do not inform us of their criteria. Moreover, they fail to acknowledge that they are acting as arbiters of appropriateness. Later in the intervention we are told that the consultants, having drawn up a report (as agreed in their contract), a report which is 'equally critical of all three parties involved, the Board, the Commissioner, and the Department as a whole', unilaterally decide 'to present their findings informally', not to the Board of Health, their 'client', but to senior officials of the City Council, the Mayor and three members of the Council's Human Resource Committee, via a series of 'informal meetings'. Not surprisingly we discover that 'the Councilmen were grateful for this early sharing of the feedback by the consultants'.

The decision to give a preview of the report to a central and politically powerful committee on the City Council a week before submitting it to their clients was only taken after 'many hours of discussion'. We are told that the reason for so doing was that the consultants felt there was a danger that the report would gather dust in a filing cabinet and have no effect on improving the efficiency of the department. On those grounds they unilaterally decided to redefine their client as the larger community, the City of Cincinnati as represented by its senior officials. How the authors reconciled such a power play with their ideals of openness and trust is not made clear. What is clear is that in this instance the consultants did not practise what they preached.

Worse still, in the present context, they do not face up to and explore the implications of their actual strategy nor attempt to reconcile it with the broader body of OD thinking. This would entail not only accepting, for example, the political nature of the consultants' activities, but also actively developing concepts around these aspects of the role. This may create some discomfort for the authors in view of the heady ideals and values that were the hallmark of the genesis of the OD movement, but we regard it as preferable to a stance which is handicapping the process of learning. As one of our research subjects commented:

> Anybody who wrote anything about the state of OD in this country, if it wasn't disparaging, then I would feel that it wasn't quite genuine because it is a disparaging business.

Use of Concepts

Our final reservations regarding written case descriptions of change episodes are based on broad observations about the way in which terms and concepts are used by authors and about some of the implications of such usage. We summarize our concerns by an extract from our original research proposal:

> Ill-defined terms and concepts are used in widely differing ways by different writers. This not only creates confusion and mis-representation but also devalues the 'language'. More serious perhaps is the possibility, and belief on our part that the use of existing and popular concepts may frustrate learning about change and the development of new concepts because the convenience of existing categories discourages writers from considering new categories and classifications. In brief, we believe that many accounts of planned change are moulded to fit (and reinforce) existing concepts and terminology, hence discouraging the development of new ones.

If written accounts exert a predominantly conservative influence on the development of theory and stifle creativity, we hoped that the greater spontaneity of spoken accounts would allow more scope for expressing and describing some of the insights, intuitions, and hunches of interventionists that, for us, constitute a vast yet relatively untapped reservoir of understanding about change.

Why have we written it?

We regard OD thinking and practice as an emergent field. Some have described OD as in its adolescence (Friedlander, 1976). Certainly Organization Development is less fashionable now than it was a decade ago: indeed the current fashion seems rather to be to criticize the field for any number of weaknesses and to dismiss it as an outdated fad.

Criticisms stem as much from inside the profession as from outside. Principally it has been attacked as being atheoretical, a hotch-potch of techniques and gimmicks loosely clustered around a naïve and overoptimistic set of values and assumptions about organizational man. A major weakness has been its failure to take adequate account of the politics of organizational life, preferring to regard such activities as a symptom of malaise, the cure for which lay in developing honest, open, trusting, and 'authentic' relationships such that effective communication was restored. Of late there are signs that such attitudes are changing. Certainly there is now a growing awareness of the centrality of power and politics in the process of organizational change and of the inevitability of such processes. Indeed it is possible, perhaps, to recognize a shift in attitude on the part of some OD writers and practitioners who seem to be moving away from a normative stance and adopting a more pragmatic attitude towards such activities. Instead of regarding politics as unhealthy and, by implication, 'wrong', they seem to have come to regard them as an endemic and enduring feature of organizational life such that the issue now is not, 'how can we change this state of affairs?', but instead, 'how do the political processes operate and how can they be harnessed to the change effort?'. However, accepting the inevitability of power and politics in organizations is not the same as evolving a theory for intervening in them. It is on this count that much further work is required.

In its heyday, OD spawned many practitioners. Those who have survived and succeeded in the field have done so because they worked out their own ways of compensating for the inadequacies of the subject as formally represented in the literature. In this way we consider that OD has flourished in a multitude of different directions and that there exists a vast amount of personal wisdom about facilitating organizational change. Such wisdom in many cases may be significantly different from conventional OD writing but is indebted to it for having provided a point of departure. It has been our ambition in this research to capture and describe the diversity of OD as it is currently practised.

Our ambition goes somewhat further than this, however, and relates to a previous observation that OD has been criticized on the grounds that it is atheoretical. Friedlander and Brown in 1974 made the observation that:

> OD today is a long way from being the general theory and technology of planned social systems change we would like to see it become.

In 1976 Beer spelt out some of the requirements for such a theory as he saw it:

> This theory should provide a better understanding of how and when various technologies are applicable and how they can be integrated. In the meantime OD technology provides applied behavioural scientists with powerful tools for changing organizations. These tools go far beyond applied research, the primary means for changing organizations in the past.

Finally, a somewhat more scathing opinion from Strauss (1976):

> At times OD is little more than abstract moralization masquerading as scientific theory. Even at best we have a theory of change agent intervention, not a theory of planned change.

In our view one of the reasons for the lack of such a theory is the paucity of concepts available to the would-be theorist and the inadequacy of such concepts as are available. The forms and concepts in use are, for the most part, imprecise and ambiguously used, a point made by Kahn (1974):

> Scientific research and exploration requires concepts that get beneath convenient labels and observable events and behaviours. The literature of organization development is disappointing in this respect; it is tied too closely to the labels in terms of which the varied services of organizational development are packaged and marketed. One of the persisting problems with research on organizational change is that it has incorporated such colloquial and commercial terms as independent variables.

We share Kahn's disappointment concerning the quality of concepts in OD. Without more rigorously defined concepts that are both 'grounded' in the actual practices of interventionists and internally coherent or 'robust' in themselves, we see little chance of developing theories at a higher level of generalization with any degree of confidence. Deriving concepts that have their foundations in the repeated patterns of actual change projects is an important task toward the possibility of constructing a theory or theories of change therefore, and represents one of our main ambitions both for the research and in this book.

Finally, we wish to re-evaluate some of the 'sacred cows' of the OD literature in the light of current practice. In particular we are interested in such notions as *planned change*; the extent to which practitioners operate according to the *truth/love model of orgazational change* based on the values of openness, authenticity, and trust; and the notion of a *collaborative approach* to organizational change with the *interventionist as a neutral facilitator* and helper. Also we are interested in the way in which OD projects begin. In particular we look at the notion, popular in the literature, of *felt need* as the starting point for an intervention.

How the Book has been Written

Each main chapter has been written by one member of the research team according to his particular area of interest, and in consultation with the other members. Consequently the style of writing varies between chapters. We considered that while this may contravene the normal practice in co-authored publications it was preferable to what would have been a contrived uniformity in style. In our opinion, this would have been contrary to the spirit in which the research was conducted and indeed to one of the themes of the findings, namely that of diversity.

The reader may notice that, on occasions, the same quotation is used in more than one chapter and to illustrate different points. We simply wish to declare that this is deliberate and not the result of careless editorial scrutiny.

In the next chapter, David Sims outlines the methods that were used to collect and analyse our basic data, and explains some of the problems that this created together with our methods of either resolving or living with them.

Chapter 3, by Adrian McLean, describes the roles played by expert consultants in the process of organizational change. The general theme is that their roles are far more complex and varied than is commonly portrayed in the literature. In particular, consideration is given to the link between external (independent) consultants and those internal to specific organizations, with an emphasis on the complementarity of these roles.

Chapter 4, written by Iain Mangham, examines the political activities of change agents, an area much neglected in descriptions of their roles hitherto. Here we present our findings that some interventionists do not operate according to the standard OD model of openness, honesty, and clarity. Far from accepting OD values such as consensus and collaboration, many people seem (consciously or unconsciously) to be operating from a more political set of values. The chapter suggests a model of interpersonal behaviour based on a dramaturgical analogy, argues that the role of the expert is to bring about 'negotiated changes', and compares his activities to a Machiavellian model.

Chapter 5, by David Sims, describes some of the ways in which consultants are invited in. Data from the research are examined in order to generate some tentative theories about the derivation of the issues which are used to define interventions. These data are contrasted and compared with the expectations set up in some of the literature, and consideration is given to the implications of our findings for some traditional assumptions regarding consulting practice.

In *Chapter 6*, David Tuffield looks at the key concept of 'planned change'. Various definitions are considered. He presents and discusses our findings with regard to this central concept, in particular the paradox that much of the change brought about by experts is not planned (in the conventional sense of the term) and that those who engage in the most planning appear to accomplish little change.

In *Chapter 7*, Adrian McLean presents a continuum of consultant behaviour based on its proximity to either of two extreme poles, Centred and Un-integrated, and examines the significance of these ideas for the future of OD generally and the development of practitioners in particular.

Conclusion

At the time of writing, people seem to be losing faith with Organization Development. Much of the characteristic energy and optimism of its practitioners is dissipating. One explanation of this state of affairs may be quite simply that OD has lost its relevance. Confronted by the harsh political, social, and economic facts of contemporary life, there is generally less tolerance for what are sometimes seen as indulgent, expensive, and time-consuming processes of introspection and development. The current preference is for action, not reflection. Organizations and governments seem to be more concerned with survival than with development; with firm

8

leadership rather than consultation and negotiation. These trends are accompanied by, and may be a result of, a clear shift in the balance of power away from the shop floor, the individual employee, and the trade unions, in favour of those people in senior and centralized positions of power.

Rooted as it has been in assumptions of a more consensual and collaborative approach to decision making, and in the hippy culture of the late 1960s, OD may be in danger of suffering the ultimate indignity of failure to adapt to changes in its environment.

An alternative interpretation, and one that we prefer is that there are signs of a metamorphosis within OD, a shedding of the skin of the late sixties and a transformation into a creature far better adapted to the harsher realities of the 1980s but with a wisdom retained from its earlier form. Moreover, we see a danger of over-reaction; that in mourning the demise of OD in its traditional form we pay insufficient attention to those lessons that we have learned as a result of the experiment, and fail to recognize and nurture newly emerging practice. This book is an attempt to focus in on the lessons learned.

References

Beer, S. (1976). The technology of organization development. In Dunnette, M. D. (ed.), *Handbook of Industrial and Organizational Psychology*, Chicago: Rand McNally, 937–992.

Friedlander, F. (1976). OD reaches adolescence: an exploration of the underlying values. *Journal of Applied Behavioural Science*, **12**, 7–21.

Friedlander, F., and Brown, L. D. (1974). Organization development. *Annual Review of Psychology*, **25**, 313–341.

Goodstein, L. D., and Boyer, R. K. (1972). Crisis intervention in a municipal agency: A conceptual case history. *Journal of Applied Behavioural Science*, **8**, 318–401.

Kahn, R. L. (1974). Organization development, some problems and proposals. *Journal of Applied Behavioural Science*, **7**, No. 3, 485–502.

McLean, A., Hyder, S., Mangham, I., Sims, D., and Tuffield, D. (1980). *Implications of Interventions in Organizations*, Chemical and Allied Products Industry Training Board, Basingstoke, England.

Strauss, G. (1976). Organization development. In *Handbook of Work Organization and Society*, Chicago: Rand McNally, 617–684.

Chapter 2

The Methodological Framework
of the Research

Our object in this chapter is to explain how we came to do what we did in the way
that we did it, in order to be clear about what we do and do not think we can claim
to have found out. We believe that the methodologies employed in a piece of
research affect the kinds of knowledge that emerge — both in the content of that
knowledge and also in the way that it should be understood and used by readers.

We shall begin by describing the overall criteria that we think guided us in
our consideration of methodologies. Then we shall describe the procedures
that we actually followed in conducting the research. Finally we shall discuss
the principal methodological questions that we had to contend with as we
sought to follow our criteria in this piece of research.

Our Criteria for a Methodology

In retrospect, there were several criteria for what we would have taken to be
satisfactory processes and outcomes for this research which had to be met by
the methodology we used. Although we handled methodological questions
mostly in an incidental and implicit way, as a group of researchers who trusted
each others' rigour and responsibility without expecting to be able to agree a
new standard of methodological orthodoxy, our emerging methodologies had
to be reviewed in the light of these criteria until the research team felt satisfied
with them. We do not claim to have discussed the criteria beforehand, or that
we have fully met any of them, but we do claim substantially to have
approached them. There were five particularly significant criteria.

1. *The research should be comprehensible* to the consultants, clients, and
   patients whose accounts of their experiences of interventions in organizations were used as data. This applied both while we were talking to them,
   when we wanted them to understand what we were doing so that they could
   make judgements within their own expertise about what they should tell us
   about; and after we had finished, so that they would tell us if we had
   understood them correctly. At no point was there a realistic hope that the
   research might be fully endogenous (Maruyama, 1974); it was, however, the
   view of the research team that an investigation which was incomprehensible

9

to the persons whose experience, behaviour and theories were being investigated was highly unlikely to reveal those aspects of the topic that were of most importance to those persons. Such an investigation, conducted without concern for comprehensibility, could employ concepts of processes and of events which could be easily related to other parts of the academic literature, but it was our view that satisfactory validation of the research could only come about if the terms used, and hence the account given, were comprehensible to our collaborators in the research; only they could say if the findings matched their experience, as opposed to merely reconfirming the framework of the researcher. The research should therefore be 'grounded' (Glaser and Strauss, 1967; Glaser, 1978) in the concepts and beliefs of those involved in organizational interventions; that is, it should be built around the concepts, beliefs, and theories that were used by consultants to guide their interventions, rather than being couched in the rather different terms used in much academic description. This leads us to approach our task in the opposite manner to, for example, White and Mitchell (1976), in whose paper 'a logical classification system for independent and dependent variables frequently employed in OD is proposed' (p.57).

2. *The research should be academically acceptable.* The research team was situated organizationally in a university, and so there were norms of rigour and carefulness, of making the findings available in a way which would permit them to be understood and evaluated by other members of the academic community, and of taking critical cognizance of the pre-existing academic work in this and related fields. A certain (if indefinable) level of academic acceptability would be adequate; anything less than this level would create problems for us in our organization, but anything more would not produce additional pay-offs of significance to the research team, whilst it most probably would begin to produce conflicts with criterion 1.

3. *The methodology should be appropriate to the topic.* Most of the rest of this chapter is devoted to our efforts to fulfil this criterion. For the present it will be sufficient to say that it was important that the methodology should exclude as little of the complexity of the topic as possible, and that it should be as open as possible to any necessary reconstruction of the researchers' theoretical framework as the investigation proceeded. In fact this criterion was not only about appropriateness to the topic, but also about flexibility, so that we should not be constrained from redefining the topic as the research proceeded and as we learned more.

4. *The methodology should be consistent with the researchers' model of man.* The research team followed the dictum of the anthropomorphic model of man that 'we should treat people, for scientific purposes, *as if they were human beings*, as we know and understand them in everyday life' (Harre and Secord, 1972, p.87). The crucial feature of this model in the present context is that human beings are distinguished from other objects of scientific enquiry by their self-awareness. '. . . a human being is a system

of a different order of complexity from any other existing system, natural or artificial. We believe this to be evident in the fact of human self-awareness and in the characteristically human linguistic powers. Thus for the purpose of any science which deals with phenomena specifically associated with performances that depend upon these higher order capacities any model of less complexity is void'. We found that we needed a methodology which deliberately encouraged people to give us accounts about their self-awareness; otherwise we would not be getting a full report about their perceptions, experiences, and actions. Even amongst OD practitioners it seems that it is not necessarily seen as legitimate to include your self and your awareness in your accounts of situations.

5. *The research should be useful* to some members of, and some consultants to, organizations. The research should have explanatory value for organization members and for practising consultants to teams. This was important for two reasons, the first historical and the second methodological.

Firstly, the historical reason was that the research was funded by the Chemical and Allied Products Industrial Training Board, and the Board's officers had argued in favour of funding the research on the grounds that, amongst other things, the research would be useful to their Management Advisory Unit, and that they would expect advances in understanding to be shared with the industry. This coincided with our view as a research team that the topic was worth investigating because we ourselves had met situations when intervening in organizations where we would have found a better understanding of the topic useful.

Secondly, the methodological reason behind this criterion had to do with validation. For an investigation conducted outside the paradigms of traditional behavioural and organizational research the issue of validation, which is commonly solved within those paradigms by an appeal to tradition or by showing that the findings fit well with the existing corpus of findings, becomes problematic. With the rather different paradigm employed here, the test for validity becomes 'Does the work show itself to be valid in the work experience of organization members and consultants?'. Also, for a person to supply good qualitative data to a researcher is a time-consuming and effortful business; organization members are not likely to be motivated to give good accounts unless they can see potential usefulness in the study.

These two reasons are drawn together in a remark by Dunn and Swierczek (1977):

> Grounded theory, then, means continuous efforts to relate existing concepts, methods and practices such that 'experience' in its widest sense becomes available for public discussion (p.137).

This list of criteria is not exhaustive. Such matters as time, money, access, and the experiences and preoccupations of the researchers have not been mentioned. However, the criteria listed above were the chief criteria that we had become aware of having used by the end of the research; other criteria not in the list probably operated in the different fashion of preventing methodologies from consideration.

The Procedure We Followed

In this section we shall discuss how we got started, how we conducted interviews, and how we did our analysis.

Getting Started

In the initial stage of the main project we built up a card index file of people currently involved in trying to bring about organizational changes (of a behavioural rather than a technological nature) in the chemical industry. The file was developed on the snowball principle — by telephoning people whom we knew to be involved and getting them to put us in touch with relevant others. This had a number of advantages over, say, a postal survey to chemical companies:

— we got straight to a suitable person
— we could make immediate personal contact with potential participants in the research
— we could learn in more detail about the sorts of change programmes or interventions in progress than we could have done from responses to a standardized questionnaire.

We were able to check the scope of our index in various ways: for example, against the membership list of relevant societies and networks, through our contact with various Board staff and with researchers in the same field from other universities. We also discussed current trends in organizational change and development with colleagues who are researching or consulting in different industries and different countries.

The intention behind this sort of informal survey was for us to get a broad picture of the direction and main trends in the making of organizational interventions in the chemical industry, where such activity was concentrated, and who was involved. We then selected a small number of cases to follow up in depth on the basis of criteria such as:

large multinational companies	*versus*	medium sized/smaller companies
interventionist based at head office	*versus*	interventionist based out in manufacturing companies
focus on an external interventionist	*versus*	focus on an internal interventionist

We wanted to make sure that all these categories were covered in our data collection, although we did not make the assumption that they should become important dimensions for analysis, and in fact only the third category did.

Our choice of cases was also influenced of course by practical considerations such as the distance involved and people's willingness to participate. Gaining commitment to the research turned out to be relatively easy (perhaps because organization development is supposed to be a helping profession) and most participants were interested in taking up our offer to share our findings with them at a later stage.

Interviews

Apart from some documents from participants, all the fieldwork consisted of interviews. In the main study, these interviews were conducted on the following principles, which had been developed in pilot studies:

— The aim was to discover grounded theory (Glaser and Strauss, 1967) and not to prove or disprove specific hypotheses;
— the emphasis was on the participant's own involvement in the change programme: on what he said he had done, was doing, and expected to do or to happen; and on his underlying philosophy and the beliefs which chiefly influenced his behaviour;
— within broad bounds, we wanted the participant to tell us what he thought was important;
— in the first interviews we aimed for as typical a picture as possible of the interventionist's main work activities and his thinking about them;
— in follow-up interviews we asked participants also to predict what they thought would happen at specific events and why, and afterwards checked back with them on these predictions.

With one or two exceptions all interviews were tape-recorded and we often interviewed in pairs because of the advantage of having two people to probe the implications of what the participant was saying, one person listening while the other framed the next question.

Analysis

We decided that the data analysis should be carried out by all team members jointly, in order to get the widest spectrum of views, and we began the process soon after the fieldwork was started. This meant that our methodology and emerging findings could be refined and tested as we went along. The analysis consisted of seven stages:

— immersion in the data (all team members listening to the interview tapes with written transcripts to hand);

— brainstorming ideas about significant points arising from each interview;
— carrying out a critique of these ideas and developing and building theories around them;
— sorting and labelling the ideas and theories, trying to find the most helpful and illuminating ways of organizing them;
— individual researchers taking away and working further with those emergent categories that seemed of particular importance to them;
— attempting to organize our findings in debate with one another, involving us in trying to make overall sense of the research categories;
— taking our findings back to the persons from whom we collected data, to see if they considered that we had come up with an accurate and useful way of understanding the situations they described to us.

These stages are, of course, iterative rather than linearly sequential. We never had the luxury of feeling sure that, because we had reached stage 6, we would not need to go back and do stage 2 again.

Methodological Questions arising in this Project

In the preceding sections we have considered some of the general criteria which needed to be satisfied by the methodology used for this project, and the details of the procedure we used. Within the overall framework we turn now to consider particular issues in methodology which arose in this research. There were nine main issues that we had to spend time debating, which may be broadly labelled:

1. Simultaneous, prospective, and retrospective accounts
2. Asking people to account for things they have not thought about before
3. Recall of events for accounts
4. Imposing logic on accounts
5. Giving accounts to fit the literature
6. The influence of the question on the accounts
7. Deciding who to interview
8. Researchers' direction of accounts
9. Understanding participants' accounts through researchers' frameworks.

Simultaneous, Prospective, and Retrospective Accounts

In trying to discover the actions (and the theories underlying those actions) taken by a person in the context of his organization under conditions usually of pressure and uncertainty, it is virtually certain that you will be unable to collect his accounts at the same moment as he is actually attempting to effect changes; even if you could, you would create such an unusual situation for a change-maker that you would need to find some way of allowing for the peculiar social situation (at least if he saw it as such) in which the presence of the researcher had placed him.

Not being able to collect accounts blow-by-blow as the changes took place was a mixed curse. Experience of data collection where it is possible to get those interviewed to give a commentary on what they are doing as they do it has shown us that such commentaries often do not come out in a way which shows the values, beliefs, and theories that are guiding the actor. In retrospective or prospective accounts, however, people are more frequently able and willing to say what will lie or did lie behind any action. The great majority of the quotations that we give from our interviewees in other chapters of this book, for example, are not the sort of statement that people might be expected to make at the same time as doing the things they are commenting on.

While of course the actor has the opportunity now to impose a logic on events which did not exist at the time, it is equally true to say that he has an opportunity to describe a logic of events which did exist at the time. He might not have been explicitly conscious of that logic, and he would not have been able to spare the time and effort for the relatively slow process of articulating it at the time. Thus retrospective and prospective accounts are at least no worse than accounts at the time of acting and we preferred them because they were more convenient to collect and avoided fouling up the organizational politicking of our collaborators, who needed all their verbalizing for conducting their intervention.

Asking People to Account for Things they have not thought about before

Given that you will have to ask all concerned in change about those changes either in retrospect or in prospect, such a question will, as we have said above, inevitably lead to thinking, theorizing and finding of a logic on the part of the person you are talking to. Compounding this problem is the existence of a body of literature in the field of organizational change, known to many of the people involved in making such change, and they may very easily find themselves, without intending any deception, describing their actions and perspectives in such a way that they make sense in the light of this body of literature.

The possible tendency of persons to describe their actions in a way which fits in with the literature is very widespread, being bound up with questions of presentation of self. If, however, the respondents are not rewarded for speaking in the traditional language of planned change, but persist in using it, then we must give them the benefit of the doubt that these are in fact the terms in which they find it most fruitful to talk about their thoughts.

Recall of Events for Accounts

Assuming that accounts must be retrospective or prospective, there is the question of how accurately practitioners are able to recall the reasons for choices they made at any point during the activity, and the factors which affected that choice. Many OD writers speak as if practitioners follow a rational and ordered course when bringing about change, but if there were no such organizing framework (which is at least possible) it would become very difficult to recall accurately the details of actions and the reasons that guided those actions.

We guarded against some of the difficulties of recall by talking to people several times where possible, and getting prospective as well as retrospective accounts. Most interviewers played an active role, suggesting, prompting, and reminding the consultant of things he had said on previous occasions about the same project. Looking at prospective and retrospective accounts of the same intervention, and at different persons giving their accounts of events to which they were all party, we did not feel that the recall problem was as serious as we had anticipated. We did not attempt any measure of this, but as human beings we felt confident that we could recognize when other human beings could not recall, as part of our everyday conversational skill.

Imposing Logic on Accounts

Because accounts are usually retrospective or prospective, they are usually simplified and rationalized in a way which imposes a relatively simple logic on to a series of events which may have had complex causes and many decision points, and which may have been the result of both intended and unintended consequences. Such accounts miss out much of the fine detail because it is 'obviously' a peculiar case, as seen by the person in it; he will thus see no reason to describe the full complexity as he saw it even if he could remember it.

The simplification which often arises in retrospective accounts was reduced by encouraging the interviewee to run on for quite a long time on any particular project, and encouraging him, when there was an option of describing the obvious or leaving it unsaid, to do the former. Of course such accounts can still never be complete, but we believe we were able to get to levels of considerable detail in most cases, although only hearing a few elements described at such levels.

As we said under the third item, in several cases, several persons from one project were interviewed. We did not take this as a cross-check for reliability in the normal sense, but its greatest value was that the meanings which lay behind words and concepts within a project were clearer to the researchers listening because they had had other descriptions and seen other uses of the same meanings. Also, for reasons not of reliability but of the complexities of a situation where several actors were playing different roles, it was valuable to get accounts from more than one of those actors, in order to get beyond an understanding of one perspective towards an understanding of the whole.

Giving Accounts to Fit the Literature

There was a particular difficulty with the use of terms in this field. Loosely or variably defined terms and concepts are used in widely differing ways by different writers. Some of these terms have got into the currency of many persons on the receiving or creating ends of organizational interventions, and the terms are so widely and freely used that it is difficult at times to discover the meaning with which any particular term is invested by the person who is using it. If you ask them what they mean by the term, they cannot easily tell you.

So far as possible, we professed ignorance of technical terms, and asked people to explain anything that was not clearly common language. This has drawbacks, however; question too often and the interviewee will (a) think the interviewer too ignorant to be worth talking to, (b) get fed up with the tedium of explaining everything, or (c) be forced out of talking in his own terms about his own world. On balance we preferred to resolve this issue by understanding terms from the context in which they were used rather than persistently demanding definitions.

The Influence of the Question on the Accounts

The type of questions that were asked were usually quite broad, but we would not claim that the questions would not have influenced respondents in their answers, even where questions were intended to be 'non-directive'. Respondents will have answered according to cues taken partly from the question and partly from the social situation as they saw it at that time between the researcher and themselves.

On the other hand we can claim that the way questions were asked avoided cueing respondents into answering only on those dimensions envisaged. Our evidence for this is that we were sometimes surprised by the lines on which a question was answered. Whatever may have been the reason for this, it showed that our expectations could be confounded.

Deciding Who to Interview

Deciding whether a change project was relevant to the research was difficult because, on the one hand, we had people using very similar words and concepts, but then apparently doing quite different things; and on the other hand, we found that we had some people not using the accepted words and concepts of organizational change and yet doing many of the same things as the practitioners (though it is inevitably difficult to find them).

In the end this question ceased to matter; most of the people available to us at least believed that they were doing something similar enough to each other for it to be understood in the same framework; and the exceptions to this were useful as cases to help us challenge the categories we developed, because if one person thought his work was quite dissimilar to another's, he was usually quite ready to say why he thought so. In this way he would articulate his own rules for relevance. 'You could go and see Tony, but I don't really think that he is what you're after because . . .'

Researchers' Direction of Accounts

The definition of relevance is a complex issue in grounded research. One view holds that only those participating in the project, when interviewed, can define what was relevant material to tell the researchers about, and thus that interviewers should restrict themselves to few and general questions in order to prime or re-energize those interviewed. The other view holds that the interviewees, faced with such ambiguity, will make guesses about what the researcher wants to hear, or what will produce the desired effect on the researcher, and will make general questions particular enough to answer by the use of such guesswork rather than by deciding what is relevant; in other words that the ambiguity makes a respondent less, not more, free to define his own relevance in the way that he is accustomed to doing with other human beings.

Our resolution of this dilemma was that fieldworkers, as experienced social actors, chose whatever degree of openness about their own definitions of relevance seemed appropriate to them with respect to the person they were talking to. They managed this in the same way as they would manage any other conversation in which they knew what outcomes they wanted, but did not want to exercise undue influence over the other party. We see this as good methodologically, because even the most experienced researcher still has more skill and experience in conducting 'conversations' than he does in conducting 'research interviews'.

Understanding Participants' Accounts Through Researchers' Frameworks

Are we as researchers bounded by our own framework? We must presumably, like all mankind, be bounded to some extent by our own framework, but that bounding is not determined and immovable.

At the beginning and the end of the project we were bounded by our own frameworks, but in the meantime those frameworks had been expanded, reshaped, had gained and lost constructs as attempts had been made to test them against our own and others' interpretations of the data which was collected. To the extent that the frameworks were changed, they cannot have been that binding on our perspectives. The five researchers involved made a conscious effort to keep each other aware of the frameworks that were being introduced by then.

During the analysis of the data, the use of some concepts that originated from the researchers' frameworks rather than from the worlds and thinking of the interviewees was inevitable. Our view was that the deliberate introduction of researcher concepts is more likely to lead to discovery of the beliefs and ideas of the collaborator than is an attempt to discover those ideas and beliefs without using any concepts that originate from the researchers. The latter must be an illusion, even if only the interviewee's words are used. The idea that grounded concepts could be 'discovered', as if the researcher had no framework of his own with which to perceive things, is naïve.

Conclusion

Throughout this research we have faced issues and made decisions about the way in which we collected and analysed information, conscious of the fact that different methods would lead to different types of data and probably different findings and that our approach could not align closely with some of the traditional research designs in the social sciences. Our methods have been guided by beliefs and values relating not only to the field of organizational change itself, but also to the nature of the process of discovery: how new concepts, ideas, and theories are developed. It has therefore been necessary to state our position on some of these issues.

We believe that no-one can ever embark on a piece of research as an indifferent and unbiased observer, and we do not claim that our ideas in any sense constitute an objective or definitive description of the process of intervention. This is partly because we believe that ideas, techniques, and approaches are in a constant state of evolution so that even if it were possible to capture the 'reality' of current practice such a picture would quickly pass into the realms of an historical documentary. Secondly and more fundamentally from our point of view it has to do with our view of explanation in social science. We consider that any social situation can be understood, or explained, in a way that 'makes sense' using a variety of quite different analytical devices. Thus a soccer match between two professional teams can be explained using any one of several frameworks for analysis; as a leisure activity, as a form of ritualized aggression between rival religious factions, as a commercial enterprise, as a platform for political propoganda, and so on. Indeed it may be possible to make a case that it is all of these things simultaneously, and that as we invoke each new explanation so we extend our understanding to include a different dimension, a new framework. No single explanation by itself tells the complete story: at different times different explanations become more prominent, sometimes with one explanation being displaced by a different one which offers a more convincing explanation for events. Much debate and intellectual in-fighting may accompany such a revision and indeed we regard many of the epistemological debates within the social sciences as encounters between different competitors in their attempts to assert the superiority of their approaches to explanation and definition.

In the present context we see our task as that of adding to the range of explanation and frameworks for understanding the change process in general and the activities of the interventionist in particular. Our purpose is to provide alternative explanations in order to permit the student or practitioner of change a choice of frameworks for making sense of a situation.

Our previous acquaintance with the subject, both as academics and practitioners, has led us to mistrust written accounts of change. Many may be oversimplistic generalizations and a few, at worst, are fantasy. One consequence has been that we more readily noticed things which conflicted with conventional writing than those which confirmed it. Having recognized this particular source of bias however, we sought to safeguard against it to some extent, although at the same time we were aware that new insights were more likely to be found by examining discrepancies. Our findings reflect this emphasis.

Our chosen method of periodic in-depth interviews with a range of practitioners in different parts of the industry required enormous amounts of time spent in data analysis. Our findings therefore reflect an intensive study of a relatively small, although varied, segment of the total possible field. This approach was founded on our belief that more fundamental discoveries can only be made through paying close attention to the fine detail of a person's experience and things which might initially be assessed as insignificant by an outsider. This has important consequences for the status of our findings in terms of their truth, accuracy, or validity. We do not, and would not wish to, claim that our findings are representative or that they are basic truths. We regard them, however, as a step towards a more complete and broader understanding of the process of change and particularly of the role of the specialist as a facilitator of change. Our findings are an attempt to make better sense of the patterns of activity that were described to us than that which could be provided by the existing body of literature. We know that they perform this function for many of the people we talked to, and we believe they will for others. We do not believe that our findings constitute a final, definitive, or objective description of reality but that they serve as possible explanations which can help both practitioners when thinking about their roles, and members of organizations involved in intervention programmes.

References

Dunn, W. N., and Swierczek, F. W. (1977). Planned organizational change: toward grounded theory. *Journal of Applied Behavioural Science*, **13**, 2, 135–157.

Glaser, B. G. (1978). *Theoretical Sensitivity*, San Francisco: Sociology Press.

Glaser, B. G., and Strauss, A. L. (1967). *The Discovery of Grounded theory*, Chicago: Aldine.

Harre, R., and Secord, P. F. (1972). *The Explanation of Social Behaviour*, Oxford: Blackwell.

Maruyama, M. (1974). Endogenous research *vs.* 'experts' from outside. *Futures,* **6**, 389–394.

White, S. E., and Mitchell, T. R. (1976). Organization Development: a review of research content and research design. *Academy of Management Review*, **1**, 2, 57–73.

Chapter 3

Consultant Roles in Organizational Change

In this chapter we present our ideas concerning the role of expert interventionists in terms of contrasts and comparisons with the early OD literature. We do this for two main reasons. First, because the ideas governing current practice have grown out of a reappraisal of these ideas, and second, as a device to highlight the difference between theories in use and espoused theories. In order to make these comparisons, we must first describe the role of the interventionist as it is portrayed by this literature.

The Classic OD Role

A common view of change consultants to be found in the literature is that of relatively neutral facilitators adopting an open, non-prescriptive stance in order to encourage people to pay attention to the patterns of their own behaviour, to learn from their observations in order to become more sensitive about themselves and others, and to exercise more conscious choices about their own behaviour. This view was particularly strong in the writing of influential North American authors and was based on a cluster of values closely related to a humanistic and an optimistic view of organizational man's motives.

The following quotation from Fordyce and Weil (1971) typifies many descriptions of the interventionist's role. The interventionist acts in order to:

> help it (the client) to explore its everyday conduct and to *assist* it in defining how it wishes to change and how it will go about making the change. (our emphasis)

and to:

> guide the parties toward more self sufficient behaviour in solving their problems, not to make them dependent on him for decisions.

In other words as in this example, the consultant's role is often described as that of a catalyst or facilitator, creating opportunities for organizational members to collaborate with each other in diagnosing problems and searching for solutions.

21

The following comments from those we interviewed are in line with these descriptions:

> I help them (the clients) become more skilled at diagnosing.

> I feel it is important that the client I'm working with owns the problem.

> It is important to start from where they are, from felt problems.

The importance of open, trusting, and 'authentic' relationships is a defining characteristic of such writing, as in the following examples from Fordyce and Weil:

> Relationships are honest. People do care about one another and do not feel alone.

> There is a high degree of trust among people and a sense of freedom and responsibility.

An emphasis on drawing people's attention to the process by which people work together in the day-to-day life of an organization is also a familiar theme portraying the role of a change agent. His task is to encourage people to examine some of the personal and shared values and assumptions concerning the operation of an organization and to prompt them to confront differences. Ideally the consultant does this in an opportunist fashion, drawing attention to process issues as and when they arise in the natural course of events. This is often described by the phrase 'in the here and now'.

Moreover the consultant's task is described as encouraging people to question their taken-for-granted assumptions regarding their company, jobs, colleagues, and so on and to help them think through the implications of some of their planned actions.

Encouraging self-reliance and independence of the client from the consultant is another central theme to be found in the core literature. This has to do with the notion that one of the ultimate and over-riding goals of the consultant is to ensure his own redundancy in the organization by developing within it sufficient awareness and understanding of the process of change and human behaviour and by nurturing the necessary associated skills. Such skills include those of process awareness and third party consultation. This aspect of the OD role has been described as 'do-it-yourself consultancy', and is also captured by the phrase 'learning how to learn'.

Set against such a template, the picture, or more accurately, pictures of the roles played by consultants that emerged from our analysis indicate considerable discrepancies.

In the following pages we shall attempt to demonstrate that the accounts given by those whom we interviewed indicate that literature-based descriptions of the role of change specialists do little justice to the complexity and variety of roles in actual practice. Before describing what roles are apparently taken, however, we shall illustrate some of the more stark contrasts that we encountered.

Some Discrepancies

Consultant as Expert

The following statement by a consultant is in terms distinctly different from typical portrayals of the role, in as much as he considers it both legitimate and necessary to make an expert diagnosis without necessarily collaborating with the client, and to take a non-neutral interpretative stance:

> I observe what has happened, I collect information about what has happened, I feed back, I interpret, I explain. I occasionally offer models and sometimes theories but never prescriptions . . . They (the clients) actually want me in an interpretative role and an educational role, feeding in knowledge about what other people are doing, and possible ways of doing what they want to do, which I'm quite happy with because I've never bought this non-interventionist Rogerian pure model. I believe that non-intervention/non-directive counselling is a contradiction in terms.

Client Independence

Another example of the discrepancy between our findings and written descriptions of the consultant's role has to do with the frequently stated notion that his job is to help the client to learn, thereby enhancing his awareness and encouraging him to act independently of the consultant. The following statements tell a different story:

> The short term strategy is to try and describe and explain what is happening. I tried to give them an interpretation of what was going on.

> I said several times during the day that I thought the whole question now was the authority of the steering group.

> I make sure that in their diagnosis they cover all of these areas. I don't actually tell them this, but I make sure they do it.

And finally:

> We are in the process of making sure that they agree that this is what the project is about.

Again, these examples show the consultant behaving as if he had an expert's understanding and assessment of events (as one might expect), but moreover deliberately using his skills to lead the client to the same conclusion (while not always explaining this to the client).

Contrary to literature-based descriptions of the consultant's role, such tactics are unlikely to decrease dependency on the consultant, or indeed to enhance learning greatly.

Here is further evidence of the consultant rather than the client managing the process (and not always openly) and exercising or believing himself to exercise considerable control over events. In short, according to these and many other similar statements, the change consultant is not a neutral facilitator or catalyst but an expert actively influencing the ways in which problems are defined and, by implication, the types of solutions sought by organizational members, in a way likely to increase the client's reliance on him as an expert.

Our purpose here is not to judge how far earlier writers were right or wrong in their descriptions of change agents' roles, but rather to signal that, for some, considerable discrepancies now exist between such written accounts and current practice. Indeed such discrepancies could be regarded as an illustration of the evolution of practices and techniques in a still young field (Friedlander, 1976). The above examples were selected because they illustrate some of the more extreme contradictions between theory and practice. In other respects, however, our analysis of such roles coincides with earlier descriptions. We also believe that we have identified facets of such roles not described elsewhere.

Our use of the term 'external consultant' refers to those people who have a variety of clients in different organizations on an explicit contractual basis, and who normally spend a minor proportion of their time in any one client organization. Typically they have some form of independent base from which they operate, which is normally a consultancy firm or a teaching post in higher education. In contrast we use the term 'internal consultant' to refer to those people who are ostensibly preoccupied with the same type of issues as externals but who are full time employees of a single organization and who spend the majority of their time working in that organization, though not necessarily with the same client.

In the largest organizations the picture is a little more complex. While in our opinion this form of classification still obtains, we found that some individuals fulfil both roles, and are more difficult to categorize exclusively as either internal or external: they are internal in the sense that they are full time employees of the organization and spend a majority of their time working in that organization, but external in the sense that because of the size, complexity and geographical separateness of the conglomerate in which they work, their relationship with different units of the organization more closely resembles that of an external than an internal consultant. This is particularly so where the sub-units themselves have their own specialist internals.

We describe first the role played by external consultants, and then examine the types of internal roles that we encountered.

The Roles of External Consultants

Conceptual Stimulation

We found that one of the most characteristic aspects of the external consultant's role was that of provider of ideas, images, and conceptual stimulation. This was in two respects; to the client organization generally, outlining new possibilities, offering models and explanations, speculating on alternative possibilities for the future, and to the internal consultant in particular. Many of the internal consultants we spoke to relied on one or more external consultants for a variety of reasons. For most, the external acted as a highly valued source of concepts and imagery and provided alternative theoretical frameworks which helped the internal better to understand his organization and his role in it. As one internal described it:

> Consultants have done a lot of work developing 'open systems' packages so a lot of the stuff that we use has come direct from them. I find this a very helpful way of visualizing organizations . . . what we are trying to do is to get managers to be more integrated in the way they are managing things and try to get them to see their jobs as managing boundaries.

Referring to his senior management clients, an external remarked:

> Guys at the top are often functionally blinkered, they are not equipped with the management of change, the management of innovation, the predictive, the scanning, the open system, all that sort of conceptual stuff with their technologies and so on. They miss out lots of dope on what we would call domains in their scanning and their diagnosis. They think in rather straight lines, rather simplistic terms within their blinkers, tunnel vision, we call that.

This statement suggests that externals get their clients to see things differently not only by suggesting new *ways* of looking but also encouraging them to look in new *places*. (This aspect of the external's role is discussed more fully in Chapter Five.)

The introduction of new ideas, theories, and images often takes the more highly formalized structure of a training programme as in the following example:

> In the early days we were largely working on an educational strategy as part of that great corporate effort, and really just introducing people into behavioural sciences, social sciences and getting them aware of some of the processes that can occur in small groups, between groups and inside large organizations.

A final example:

> One of the things we looked for was how far they were aware of the environment and whether they ever looked outside, and we found that practically nobody did, or if they did it was only in a very passive way, they felt like pawns in that system.

While the external generates ideas and images and is a source of conceptual stimulation for internals, and via them the rest of the organization, he also relies on internals to keep him in touch with new developments, reactions, gossip, trends, and the climate of opinion generally inside the organization. They function as the external's eyes and ears, and provide him with a sounding-board and translation service.

Externals as Providers of World Views

In some of those organizations where we interviewed both externals and internals over a period of up to fifteen months, it became apparent that the terms and concepts used by internals incorporated more and more the key constructs of their externals.

We use what Kuhn (1962) termed 'paradigms' to describe the collection of theories or world views held by external consultants. These serve as the organizing frameworks within which their theories concerning human interaction and change are related. Thus, one external consultant's paradigm was based on viewing organizations in terms of power and politics and his interventions in a client system were reflected in his concern to identify and win over those with 'the power to defend or destroy' a project. He was also acutely sensitive to the indications from the client of how much power they would allow him. People were judged for their political astuteness and any mistake would be exploited unhesitatingly, as we see in the following extract from an interview:

> *Question:* What are you going to do about him? (Brian, the Works Manager)

> *External:* Oh, ignore him most of the time. He might be more difficult to ignore than Richard (the predecessor). Brian . . . he's not particularly astute in that he has revealed far too much in conversation as to why he is doing it, which can then be useful. For example, it is of key importance to him . . . that I am seen to approve of what they are doing. Brian explicitly stated that if, whenever we agree this, then I have to go to the UK head office and then I have to go to our European Headquarters with him, and the message has been given that if I say it's OK, then it's OK. Now, he should never have delivered that sort of information to me. But he has and I will exploit it.

Another important signal of his power in the situation is described in this extract from the same interview:

> . . . suddenly there's a whole rush of activities, which also signals that Brian's staking his reputation on the whole damn thing, and he wouldn't be doing that unless he'd got a very big go signal.

A further illustration of the centrality of power and politics in this external's world view is provided in the following extract where he is describing the role of key personnel who are strategically placed to assist the project; the internal consultant, Hugh, who is a personnel manager, and Jack, the Personnel Director:

> I'm more interested in Hugh's power dimension, because we need his power within the organization to keep the thing ticking over. Ideally, we should be using the Personnel Director, Jack, but Jack's very ineffective. Theoretically he has power, but practically he doesn't exercise it. He keeps his nose clean. So we would never have got as far as we have now if it hadn't been for Hugh. He has pushed and manoeuvred and talked and politicized and all sorts.

Over time, we noticed increasingly that the terms, concepts and ideas being used by the internal consultant on this project coincided with the external consultant's political view of organizational life. Describing his role in the project, the internal explained how he saw his own influence:

> Through my messages coinciding with someone else's intervention at a different level, going into a great mishmash, and coming back as a proposal which, as I say, would fit into a *strategy* that I'm working at, awareness of the changing outside world and how it will affect the relationships with the lowest pyramid of our organization. That's the *strategic* thing, the *tactical* thing could have been a series of consultative committees set up and all the rest of it, and that's how it started out.

'Strategy' and 'tactics', terms most immediately drawn from a military analogy, fit into an overall political paradigm of organizational life. The following two extracts further illustrate our point:

> But this is strategy and tactics, isn't it? I mean, you modify your tactical approach as you see things changing, you don't lose your overall objective.

Clearly, 'strategy and tactics' are two key constructs for this internal. Another within the same paradigm is 'negotiation', as in this piece:

I suppose this is the art of negotiation, because that's what you are doing, you're negotiating with various groups of people to get certain things done. That's what it's all about.

Each external seemed to have his own dominant, or favourite, paradigm. For some, the systems approach seemed particularly helpful; others used ideas based on Lewinian force field analysis, while still others operated according to a didactic model of master–pupil. In turn their internal counterparts favoured constructs which were consistent with such orientations. Thus we found that where Systems theory was used by the external, their internals were much concerned with locating key boundaries and with improving the quality of transactions across such boundaries. Those who worked with an external who was strongly influenced by Lewinian ideas were preoccupied with establishing a 'critical mass' of support for a policy in order to overcome the 'resistance' of the minority.

Among the implications of this phenomenon we consider two to be of particular significance, namely those to do with power and dependency.

The apparent tendency for client organizations to incorporate their consultant's way of viewing the world places the consultant in a particularly powerful position in that he or she influences not only where they look but also perhaps what they focus on within any one field of vision. It is our view that the type of power exerted by the external consultant is akin to what Lukes (1974) has described as second order power, namely a power to define relevance, to influence what people regard as important and what constructions they place on events.

We have been concentrating on the external's influence over the internal in this regard; however, we believe that the process does not end there but gradually and imperceptibly seeps into the rest of the organization via the entry afforded by the internal. This is especially the case where the internal adopts the cultivator role that is described later on in this chapter.

We discuss in Chapter 7 some of the possible consequences for the internal of uncritically adopting the terms and concepts of an external. In the present context we would simply note that there may exist some drawbacks for internals of an overly enthusiastic adoption of an external's constructs. We see these as twofold. First, the underlying or intuitive logic with which the external consultant integrates his ideas, imagery, and terminology may be lost or distorted in the process of transmission, so that the internal may be left with a set of loosely connected concepts that are difficult to comprehend and which apparently bear little resemblance to the activities that he is engaged in; or worse still that he *thinks* he understands but doesn't. More particularly we believe that many of the terms and concepts in use reflect former ideas, theories, and/or practices which the consultant has now abandoned in favour of more effective but as yet unnamed techniques. In other words the use of many of the terms may be habitual or perhaps a response to being asked about them in an interview. At the heart of our concern is the fact that, in our opinion, the field of organization development does not yet enjoy a sufficiently concise technical language to enable ideas to be transferred efficiently between people. Indeed many of our interviewees confessed that many of their actions were based more on intuitive processes than anything they could explicitly articulate. This is also discussed further in Chapter 7.

External as Sounding Board and Counsellor

External consultants were used by some to provide a more 'objective' point of view by supplying the internal with advice based on experience of similar situations in a wide range of organizations. Akin to this was the practice we encountered of using the external as a sounding board for trying out ideas. Referring to his external, one senior OD man commented:

> The biggest resource that he is that we haven't got inside is that he works with a whole lot of other places, and it's essentially what he knows about what's happening in other places. He's got a huge knack of being able to say . . . (he can listen to them talking and they're really escaping from or not raising the issue and he can say) 'I wonder whether you're talking about the same sort of thing that happened in . . .

For some internals, the external also acts as a personal counsellor, helping him explore his role in the context of his life goals. An external describing his role *vis-à-vis* some internals said:

> I have been encouraging them to go around the world, . . . to look at concepts, models, technologies, and to try to get into some situations where they might find out what skills they haven't got. While continuing to encourage Stephen to do that, trying to get him into action with me and people like me inside and outside. So he has some practical experience out of which comes confidence to take another leap into another sort of intervention. It's the only way really you can grow in confidence, I think, helping him review his world strategy, world goals and world strategy opposite client systems . . . . Helping him to look at his strategy, developing strategies for internals . . . it's a personal level, helping confidence to grow, confidence and practical experience and knowing himself.

Nurturing the development of internal consultants is a central concern to some externals. With one internal, for example, the external was concerned to help him resolve issues of identity.

> So have I got a client who wants (to be) a through and through OD man or not is the problem I face there, and if it's not, I'm into

counselling, life planning with him . . . it's sort of co-counselling with him to help him, because if he's not (a through and through OD man) he needs to be out for his own sake.

With another internal the problem for the external was of a different order:

I have to watch him. He is in danger of becoming a prima donna. He is becoming very confident, getting a lot of reinforcement and recognition. I think one of the worst enemies of an OD consultant, be they internal or external, is to have arrived as a big name. That is the point where they start dying and become obsolete . . . I'm really going to have to work very sensitively and carefully to not destroy his new found confidence too early. Like how am I going to help him continue to grow, not taking a year out on laurels.

Externals as Gurus

All of the externals that we spoke to seemed to have their own particular forms of charisma, and were often referred to as gurus by members of the client organization. According to the Oxford English Dictionary, a guru is a 'spiritual and influential teacher, a revered mentor, or head of a religious sect who acts in a grave and dignified manner'. While we would not wish to over-emphasize the analogy, we found that there are several aspects of an external's activities that bear comparison. We have already noted that, like gurus, externals are to some extent teachers, passing on new ideas, theories and models for understanding human behaviour to internal consultants and perhaps over time exerting a profound influence over the organization and its attitudes to people and the problems of managing change. At the same time, many of them appeared to be highly regarded by the organizations in which they worked and often seemed to create a climate of optimism around the possibility for change. Indeed it was not uncommon for organizational members to attribute to their external consultants extraordinary, almost mystical powers of prediction, perception, and manipulation.

Externals described the pressures from clients to accept the mantle of the wise man and make profound, shrewd, or bright observations very early in the association.

There is an expectation of an outsider that he is going to say something terribly clever . . . as an outsider you're brought in, and they watch you, and there is no way you can actually say anything; but you can feel driven in the first five minutes to make some asinine intervention and play your guitar or say something really very profound. But if you sit for two or three hours everybody gets very uncomfortable, including yourself; you think—Christ, I'm really going to have to deliver something red-hot now, in order to turn this thing around.

> The chief engineer turned to me after forty minutes and said . . .
> what do you think about it? And I'm thinking how the hell can I
> tell you what I think about it after forty minutes flat, but I knew I
> had to perform. So I said I really think you don't know what your
> problems are.

Regarding the external as guru may also explain Greiner's claim (1967) that interventions are more likely to succeed if they involve a prestigious outsider. From the external viewpoint, being cast in the role of guru is potentially advantageous in that it invests him with considerable, albeit short term, credibility, faith, and indeed power. It may be that faith in his perceived ability to effect or enable change is a crucial ingredient necessary for people to believe that change is possible, and is sufficient for them to make a serious commitment to making the change work. In the absence of an adequate theoretical framework of planned change, seeing the external as a guru may be a necessary substitute, something or someone to provide much needed reassurance and confidence. It may enable organizational members to relinquish more readily the familiar and known for the unfamiliar and unknown, to 'step into the dark'. Trusting that the guru has an understanding of the organization and of the process of change, and an ability to steer the participants successfully past the pitfalls and dangers of a particular episode may enable organization members to concentrate more easily on the day to day problems arising from the change. Like a guru, the external's presence may serve to reassure participants that the process will prove worthwhile eventually. This line of reasoning suggests that one of the most crucial functions fulfilled by the external consultant is to create and sustain a belief that change is possible such that people are prepared to embark on a project at all.

Externals as Fire Lighters

A significant amount of some externals' time and energy seemed to be invested in what we would liken to 'fire lighting' activities. By this we mean setting up projects and groups of people in various parts of an organization and infusing them with energy (stimulating debates, confronting difficult issues, encouraging individuals to experiment with new ideas and behaviour, introducing new perspectives on familiar issues), in the hope that some will catch fire and burn independently and that the heat and light generated (perhaps even the flames) will spread to the rest of the organization. External consultants thought that they were able to do this partly on the basis of high initial credibility and status, a view corroborated by some clients that we spoke to. However, as one external explained: 'You've only got fairly short credibility before they're looking for results'. In this sort of relationship, externals seemed to rely heavily on internal consultants not only to keep the embers glowing between their relatively infrequent visits, but also to keep them informed of the temperature both inside and outside project groups.

To summarize, the apparent role played by external consultants can be that of an educator, visionary, and prophet, providing new ways of seeing for organization members, and attempting at the same time to broaden their field of vision. They sometimes act as sounding boards and provide the wisdom of comparative experience of similar problems in other settings, and in so doing serve both to reassure and introduce fresh perspectives. They actively develop and manipulate their internal counterparts in the sense of a master craftsman nurturing the development of his apprentices, holding them back here, bullying them to experiment and expose themselves to more risks there, while simultaneously using them as a network of information sensors and as channels for disseminating ideas and examples. They are like gurus, colluding from time to time with the apparently strong desire of organization members to see them as demigod with superhuman abilities and understanding together with the power to ensure a safe passage, or salvation. They can be pioneers and evangelists, building and lighting beacons in various strategic and/or safe places. Whereas externals provide the initial flames, internals are the fire minders working to sustain the initial infusion of energy from the external, patiently stoking the fire and keeping the external informed of the temperature generally. Finally the external offers a broad and long term perspective, sometimes but not always with a sense of overall strategy. He supplies a general context and set of reference points for the internal which enables him to concentrate on more detailed involvement and to retain a sense of his own direction and purpose.

The Roles of Internal Consultants

There is a range of different roles played by internal consultants, and they have an even more varied set of organization labels. Only comparatively rarely do such people publicly (in terms of their own organizations) label themselves as Organization Development specialists. Some masqueraded as personnel officers, others as Management Services specialists, and yet others as trainers. On several occasions we were told that an OD label would be a positive handicap to their work. It would seem that the reasons for this go beyond the necessary expedient of not having repeatedly to explain the meaning of and (perhaps worse) the need for such an apparently esoteric luxury to one's line management colleagues. As we discuss later, considerations of public visibility, or perhaps more appropriately invisibility, are a central concern to internals. To some it is important for them to remain relatively inconspicuous.

The type of role taken by internals varied according to several circumstances. Not unnaturally, a good deal seems to depend on the personality of the internal himself. Those whose values were more concerned with the well-being and personal growth of the individuals in the system tended to occupy different roles from the political strategist whose concerns were related to more wide ranging issues of power. Perhaps of greater significance however was the extent to which the internal was self-aware, in touch with his own feelings and values. His role consequently tended to depend not only on his personality and value system, but how far he had resolved issues of personal identity in his work. We discuss this in more depth later.

A second factor which affects the role of the internal seems to hinge partly on the existence of an external. The roles of some internals can best be understood in terms of their complementarity with an external. When there is not an external, the internal's role seems to be quite different.

Thirdly the roles of both externals and internals seem to vary according to the organization in which they are set. They tailor their roles to work within the various characteristics of those organizations, including predominant value systems, the history of the organization's involvement in 'human relations' (in the broadest sense), and the norms and mores concerning 'how to get things done around here'. While economical, the term 'organizational climate' fails to capture the power of tradition and evolution which lends potency to each of the items listed above.

Finally, we must allow for the preferences and personal variations for defining and interpreting the role of the interventionist. We encountered a surprisingly wide set of interpretations of the consultant's role. We have organized our findings into four main types of role most commonly played by internal consultants; the Tactician, the Cultivator, the Loner, and the Trainer. While we present them as distinct types, this is, of course, more a device to facilitate description than any pretence that the boundaries are quite so discrete in actuality.

The Tactician

The tactician is a foil for the strategic external. He operates at the sharp end of organizational life and engages in the hand-to-hand fighting. As the metaphor implies, he operates typically within the context of an overall battle plan and is intimately involved in discussing and drawing up the details of those plans. He is much concerned with eleboate manoeuvres to gain ground and outflank opponents. Like a member of the intelligence service, his currency is information (often of a highly sensitive nature) and at times he is willing to arrange discreet exchanges and covert deals. It is important for him to establish a 'legitimate front' in the organization although his precise role, activities and allegiance may differ significantly in some respects. Fleet of foot, he is quick both to advance and retreat, and, as a member of a small elite corps, he is highly mobile, moving to exploit the greatest opportunities. He is anxious to recruit extra support and gain ground by dint of having superior numbers on his side.

As a foil for the strategic external, the tactician sits in on the committees, acts as the process consultant, conducts the interviews, writes the reports, makes the presentations, does the counselling, and runs the workshops. It is the tactician who arranges the meetings with and between key personnel and who prompts them to address the real issues. Central to the tactician's role is both a plan, a planning process and a network of colleagues with whom to design and discuss strategy. In some cases, this took the form of charts in a special chart room. These charts included such items as pressures on the business, overall organizational goal and repercussive goals and they incorporate action plans for various contingencies. Up to one or two days a month are set aside for planning meetings and tacticians set up colleague groups to devise and revise those plans.

> We call ourselves the nucleus group because we are trying to formulate OD strategy.

and on a more elaborate scale:

> The strategy group takes on where the nucleus group leaves off, the nucleus group is really where we strategize and get our plans and so on, the strategy group is designed . . . to take those on and give them some implementation and we decide there who can access what parts of the organization and how and so on.

It is through such groups that networks of internals working in large organizations maintain contact and co-ordinate their activities. They may also serve to offset the feelings of isolation, impotence, and peripherality that seem to lie close to the surface for some tacticians, as in the following comment:

> I can see these guys actually being a bit concerned about what the hell we're doing there anyway and especially if we don't make it very clear to them. Some of them will be dead against us being there just as process consultants because they'll see it as a bit of head shrinking.

Part of the planning process involves locating and marshalling personnel to spearhead important campaigns. This entails identifying key groups and powerful individuals, devising ways of gaining their support and overcoming their resistance to change:

> The project that I'm really working on at the moment is to get into the divisional top team and to build a critical mass with the top team.

As with an advancing army, the objective is apparently to set up a steady momentum which gathers pace and support as it moves until ultimately it overwhelms all opposition. Here is a further example of the use of the term 'critical mass' to express this idea:

> I use the term critical mass. There is now a critical mass in the

group which says we're for this and an important part of that critical mass is the top man himself.

What we've been doing over the past eighteen months to two years is building a readiness in the group to accept this sort of intervention.

. . . If I can get enough of the group to say 'we want to do this' because then it becomes their agenda and they do it.

Tacticians are often like stateless persons and experience both the advantages and disadvantages that go with such a condition. They become involved in a wide and varied range of activities, some of which take them outside their organization, running workshops and giving lectures. Depending on their status and reputation, their role provides them with a passe-partout throughout their organization and occasionally they have neither an immediate boss nor a specific job definition. They are free to roam the organization, the country and at times the world as a legitimate part of their job. Such freedom seems to hold as many threats as it does opportunities, however. Dangers include remaining on the fringes of decisions and groups, tagging on to someone else's project unsure of how far your presence is genuinely useful or simply tolerated. Linked to this is the need to create and sustain credibility, apparently a major preoccupation for most tacticians:

Now at the end of that time I was waiting, because he had objected to my presence in that meeting by letter to my director. So I was in a bit of a difficult position if you like in that he didn't really want me to be there.

We had a very good and successful meeting with the staff committee. For me, I think that is a very useful way of starting off the OD activity in a group like that. Then I think you've established a certain amount of credibility and legitimacy for being there which is one of the things which I feel very anxious about.

Tacticians often complained that compared to externals they felt handicapped by insufficient status:

If I feel anything as an individual, it's the feeling of 'Oh God, why am I an internal' because you know status and all those things can clutter up what you can really do as an individual.

People will use your time more effectively if you are an external . . . they will get more from you, because they are aware that they are paying for you.

Whereas external consultants generate heightened expectations and are very 'visible', the internal is not obliged by the client's expectations to do an instant 'song-and-dance act' but can afford to bide his time and wait for the opportune moment for action. As one man said, describing an internal consultant:

> Like the wily fox, he can wait and wait and suddenly pounce when
> the moment comes and remain behind his bush the rest of the time.

Tacticians resemble resistance workers in that they are operating to change a system from inside that system. They work hard to establish a 'legitimate' and 'respectable' front while sometimes seeking to accomplish more covert objectives, as in the following example:

> My own personal mission (not necessarily what the company thinks
> it is paying me for), reduced to its utmost simplicity . . . is to try
> and make human institutions work better than they do. We need
> institutions, human institutions, including large institutions, and
> therefore what I want to do is not remove them but make them
> behave better.

Thus far these sentiments are likely to be widely shared throughout the senior management of any company. An elaboration of the phrase 'behave better' reveals what could prove to be a more controversial attitude toward company policy however:

> As a multi-national company, we have enormous social and
> economic power which could be used for very good things like
> getting into the third world issues and still making a decent
> respectable profit. The third world countries are not going to make
> it unless somebody helps them. No national government can do
> that, no academic institution can do it although it can influence
> people in the very long term. The people who have the possibility of
> doing it are people like (us) because we have the existing market
> networks, political contacts, a great deal of the acceptability in
> many of these countries.

At the beginning of this section, and obliquely throughout it, we have reinforced our original assertion that consultants are not 'neutral', 'independent', or 'objective' observers who attempt to improve the efficiency of interpersonal processes, but that on occasions they are also highly active agents who deliberately seek to influence substantive issues. We have used a military analogy to describe this particular type of internal role and have hinted at, but not fully addressed, the political nature of the role. This is because we discuss the micropolitics of organizational change in the next chapter.

The Cultivator

The cultivator occupies a linking role between the external and the client organization, and as such is a crucial part of the communication chain, particularly from the external's viewpoint.

The cultivator is a sower of seeds, not indiscriminately scattering them over barren and fertile soil alike but carefully selecting the most propitious conditions before planting them with care and deliberation. He is an expert climatologist, sensitive to the slightest changes in temperatures and, as an accomplished reader of the climatic signs, can often predict future weather conditions with considerable accuracy.

Planting and nurturing ideas The cultivator acts as an information disseminator, introducing new ideas and attitudes, new approaches to thinking about issues as well as proposals for action. Generally he draws his inspiration from an external (as described earlier). The nature of this input seems to change over time from a general educative input in behavioural science ideas to more problem specific suggestions as the following internal described:

> In the early days we were largely working on an educational strategy as part of that great corporate effort, and really just introducing people into behavioural sciences, social sciences, and getting them aware of some of the processes that can occur in small groups, between groups and inside large organizations.

For more specific changes to occur, another internal described his role in the following way:

> To get any change you've got to be prepared to say something a lot of times and the key is to say it early, so that you have a little bit of time in planning. You say it to a multitude of people, starting with the internal grapevine, the bureaucracy . . . . So first, I say it to my committee here, and then I say it to the personnel director in London, and he says it to the staff committee there. Someone then goes off and talks to the man in head office and that's how it goes. The usual thing is you have got the information and fostered the idea that someone ought to be discussing it, and then six months later someone says 'Don't you think it would be a good idea if . . .?' and you say 'What a good idea! That's life, isn't it?'

In these ways the cultivator carefully sows the seeds of ideas, nurtures them throughout the organization and often over a long period of time, while at the same time ensuring that he is not seen to be too obviously campaigning for them.

Not only does the cultivator introduce ideas (often originating from the external), but he also acts as a translator, expressing them in the language of the organization. One internal describing his relationship with the external explained:

> We've got a good relationship. Steve (external) introducing new ideas, me acting as the translator of those ideas in what might be called in that department, 'transferring into action'.

A different internal described the same role:

> What you are trying to do in an organization is reflect what you believe are practical things that are applicable and appropriate to your organization. You are not wholly messianic or prophetic, or anything like that because you can't afford to be, . . . you'd never make any progress, you've no dialogue, you're not in the same track.

Cultivator as sensitive to the climate The term cultivator is used not only in the sense of a medium for the introduction and translation of ideas but it is also used to describe the reverse communication process, harvesting of information, and feeding it back to the external, or as one internal described it:

> Geoff (external) will then come and talk to me about it (his conversation with the MD) because he needs my feel for the organization, in other words I act as his eyes and ears, out into the organization a lot. So we are working very much as a pair.

Another external described his use of personnel managers as internals:

> We use the personnel managers from the separate parts of the organization as a link point or a front man. We are in the process of going around to them saying 'what is happening, is there any help you need from us?'
> I see his role (Personnel Manager) as being very much a senior and a front line diagnoser, if you like.

Knowing the people in the organization and building up a network of relationships is an activity which holds a high priority for most interventionists both internal and external. By comparison with internals the amount of time available to externals to establish such a network is severely limited however. One consultant, for example, spent only twelve days in a year with a major client. As a consequence externals depend heavily on internals as their network of information sensors, keeping them in touch with day-to-day events in the company, and providing them with a constantly revised picture of the state of the client organization. Moreover internals provide an opportunity for the external to test out ideas, to advise on what the organization would accept and what it would not, and generally to ensure that planned interventions are appropriate.

Cultivation is a patient long term business There is a third sense in which the term cultivator connotes the activities of some internal consultants; namely that of permanence, and gradual patient growth over a long period of time. Internals, as full time members of their organizations, see part of their role as helping things along; people, ideas, and activities grow painfully and almost imperceptibly slowly. One internal outlined the history of his OD role in conjunction with the external:

> In those early days . . . when we were trying to help works managers and their teams, we (internal and external) managed to make links inside. Sometimes he has been able to pick up a contact from working with a division board (member) who has moved on. Sometimes we have been able to introduce him. So there has been the two of us if you like, slowly increasing the level of contact up the hill, using, never initiating, an idea.

Later in the interview the same internal described how it took him six months to introduce a board of directors to the possibility of an alternative way of evaluating projects and reaching decisions than writing and exchanging papers on the subject, leaving the ultimate decision to the deputy chairman.

> It took us six months just slowly dripping with individuals and getting them to talk to each other about what might be the best way.

Yet another internal observed somewhat ruefully:

> The ways of affecting people (to make things happen) can be direct or they can be tortuous and long-winded, and in our organization it's long-winded. You know, it's a very slow evolving process; it's tortuous, it's a tortoise!

and later,

> My own personal role has always been, as it will continue to be, partly educational, partly catalyst, change agent, you know, it's a talk talk role.

The Loner

We encountered a small number of internal consultants who appear to be acting as 'lone operators'. (The small number should not surprise us since our interview subjects were approached on the basis of suggestions from people who were mostly linked into various colleague networks. Loners, by definition, rarely belong to such networks.) They have no apparent links with an external and take little collective action with other internals. Loners' involvement in projects is strictly limited in time and whereas cultivators would typically emphasize the continuous and seamless nature of their role, loners see their involvement more in terms of discrete, short term projects. An account of his work given by one such loner describes the care with which he planned his part in specific projects and the clarity of the role he carved out for himself. He described himself as: choosing to make an educative input on problem definition and resolution for half a day before helping the client to address a specific organizational problem the following day; acting as a third party to facilitate a role negotiation between a boss and his subordinate while being clear that part of this requires providing political protection, or acting as an umbrella; and addressing questions of process with yet a third group of managers engaged in union negotiations. This particular person appeared to be keen to establish the boundary of his usefulness and to limit the extent of his involvement, taking care to withdraw from a situation once he saw it as the province of another function or department. In comparison with the tactician, the loner seems to be less concerned with formulating plans and strategies for the future. His role is both more contingent and opportunistic.

The more specific and limited nature of a loner's involvement in projects may perhaps illumine the role played by externals in other companies. It could be that there are advantages in having both an internal and an external consultant in a change project; one to take a broad and long term perspective and to concern himself with strategic planning, leaving the other free to become immersed in the detail of small-scale specific projects.

Developing high levels of trust with an extensive network of personal relationships at all levels of the organization was emphasized by all consultants both internal and external. For loners, however, it was of paramount importance:

> For me it is very important that if you are working as an internal OD man you need to evolve quite strong relationships . . . The notion of trust too . . . that what you say to the OD man will go no further unless you want it to go further.

Paradoxically the impression gained in the course of interviewing these people was that they are 'loners' only in a technical or professional sense. We were struck by their apparent intimate and friendly relationships with a wide range of organization members.

The Trainer

As the label suggests, trainers are predominantly involved in devising, designing and running courses ranging from T-groups, introductions to transactional analysis, and Blake and Mouton's Grid (1964) to tailor-designed courses on human relations and interactive skills. We include them in our classification because several of those to whom we had been directed as being involved in OD were mainly concerned with training.

We found ourselves wondering how far such trainers fell within the scope of our study, but decided to include some of them because many organizations use training programmes and packages as a prelude to more problem specific OD activities, and regard them as an integral part of the OD effort.

On many occasions we encountered an attitude of ambivalence towards training on the part of both internals and externals. Whereas many saw it as indispensable to heightening levels of sensitivity and awareness on the part of organizational members, they also regarded it as a seductive substitute for 'real OD', namely working on line issues as and when they arose. The trainer is seen as having more power to control and constrain events than an OD practitioner working on 'live' issues. He enjoys the comfort and drawbacks of an institutionalized role that has gained increasing legitimacy in the last fifteen years, and is likely to experience fewer problems of credibility and identity than the Tactician, the Cultivator, and the Loner. On the other hand he must endure the impotence and bureaucratic encumbrances of a publicly account-able and acceptable role. For some, the trainer role is a transitionary status, along the route toward becoming an OD practitioner.

Our fundamental concern about the trainer role in the context of OD, however, is that it can become an OD cul-de-sac both for the occupant and his organization, a tempting distraction from facing the often uncomfortable facts of organizational life. We fear that managers and trainers may too often set up a sophisticated series of highly professional training events which are immensely stimulating for participants and rewarding for the trainers both emotionally and politically, but which ultimately and inevitably can become a diversion from tackling the difficult and enduring interpersonal problems inherent in all organizations. This is not to say that it doesn't have a legitimate role in its own right. While training is an essential stage for most companies seriously involved in OD, it can easily become an end in itself and a major obstacle to working on current problems facing an organization.

Internal consultants occupy a variety of different roles. We have portrayed what we see as four of the most characteristic such roles; the Tactician, more con-spicuous than most; his activities are perhaps best understood when seen in the context of an overall plan. The Cultivator is more characterized by his patience, permanence, and by the fact that he is almost imperceptible against the overall background of the organization. Solitude, clarity, and independence are the hall-marks of the Loner, whereas the Trainer is a man with feet in two camps, and as a consequence may be handicapped by a failure to commit himself fully to either.

We have deliberately (although not always successfully), attempted to refrain from evaluating the relative effectiveness of the types of consultant roles that we have described in this chapter. This is for two reasons. First, we see our business as *describing* what emerged from our analysis of taped interviews with these people. We leave it to our readers to decide for themselves the appropriateness of various roles depending on the type of organization being considered. Secondly, the effectiveness of any particularly role can only be judged by the extent to which it is appropriate to the organizational setting in which it exists. This includes not only questions of organizational culture, but also, and importantly, the organization's history of involvement in OD. Different roles may be appropriate at different times. Moreover, criteria of effectiveness are ultimately a question of personal beliefs and values.

We would remind the reader that the range of roles described here are not quiet so clear-cut or discrete in practice. Some people can and do occupy different roles at different times and occasionally seem to hold two or more roles simultaneously.

It would seem that, over the last decade, the role of OD expert has developed outward from its early descriptions and has flourished in a variety of forms and in a number of directions. One such direction has been toward a heightened realization of organizational politics and of the implications for the OD role of this fact. It is to such a discussion that we now turn.

References

Blake, R., and Mouton, J. S. (1964). *The Management Grid*, Houston, Texas: Gulf.

Fordyce, J. K., and Weil, R. (1971). *Managing with People*, Reading, Massachusetts: Addison-Wesley.

Friedlander, F. (1976). OD reaches adolescence: an exploration of the underlying values. *Journal of Applied Behavioural Science*, **12**, 7–12.

Greiner, L. (1967). Patterns of organizational change. *Harvard Business Review*, **45**, 119–128.

Kuhn, J. S. (1962). *The Structure of Scientific Revolutions*, University of Chicago Press: Phoenix Books.

Lukes, S. (1974). *Power: A Radical View*, London: Macmillan Press.

Chapter 4

A Micropolitical Perspective

> One of the most important things to me was your bit on politics . . . . The reality of organizational life is power and politics. If we are involved in change, we're involved in politics . . . if the change agent is to be effective they actually have to be involved in the politics of an organization.

> I don't use the power structure very much because that's frighteningly ineffective usually; to try to get someone to crack down on someone else — you get those kind of win–lose positions and I don't have to tell you that's not part of OD anyway.

No section of our report generated more heat and less light than the one on the micropolitics of organizational change. Some to whom it was shown in early drafts considered that, like Queen Victoria's bloomers, it should not see the light of day. Others argued that it would do a grave disservice to those in the profession, in effect it could make their job more difficult, presumably because professionals are to be regarded as above politics. Still others regarded the tone of this section of the report as particularly 'cynical' or 'disparaging'. On the other side were ranged those who regarded the discussion of politics — thin though it is — as central and thoroughly worthwhile.

> I support you wholeheartedly. I think OD people were trapped very early on by . . . a whole lot of concepts, one of which was the rightness, if not the righteousness, of openness. I see openness and trust and those things as good values to be aimed for. They are where you are trying to move towards, but you don't do it at the expense of those within the organization, because that can happen. So I agree entirely with you that the emphasis has got to be on *political* life within particular *political* entities.

> I'm not sure if I'm making myself clear, but I feel very strongly that (a) politics is a central issue and if change agents are going to do *anything* they have to understand that, and (b) accept that they are part of it.

From the data we gathered and analysed and, most particularly, from

43

conversations we had with people after the circulation of our draft report, it emerged that there were a number of interventionists, mostly but not exclusively internals, who were seen to be successful in bringing about change but who did not operate on the 'received' model of openness, frankness, consensus, and the like. Such people seemed, consciously or unconsciously, to be operating on the basis of quite a different framework. From the discussions we had with them they appeared to subscribe to a set of ideas (as yet, in many cases, only half-formed) which depicts organizational life as a series of arenas within which members struggle and manoeuvre to have their views prevail. Not —please note—that all was deceit and deception, manipulation and subterfuge; many appeared to be claiming nothing more nor less than that men in organizations often share power and often differ about what must be done. Any discussion, therefore, is, or may be seen, as the outcome of different individuals, and groups, pulling in different directions (Allison, 1974). In this respect, those who hold such views appear to be closer to the framework outlined by Cyert and March (1969) than to that adopted by the 'classic' writers in the field of Organization Development. From the 'political' perspective, organizations are coalitions of various interests. Employees, shareholders, managers, customers, suppliers, committees, and government departments all impinge upon the organization; within it, personnel people, engineers, accountants, marketing persons, production workers, and so on also have interests. Each group may have a distinct and different set of preferences for organizational action and each group operates different criteria for the evaluation of organizational outcomes. What is good for marketing is not necessarily so characterized by production; what suits the employees may not coincide with the preferences of the shareholders.

What is more, interventionists of this persuasion appeared to accept that decisions and actions occur not solely as the result of organizational routines and procedures, nor simply as a consequence of the application of logic or reason, but also as an outcome of the power and the skills of the proponents and opponents of the decision or action in question.

It can be argued that the activities of individuals and groups within enterprises are inherently political; a process in which one or more individuals attempts to define a situation or negotiate order in such a way that their individual goals are promoted. Further it can be argued that this process is not peculiar to organizations; it may be seen as a basic one underpinning all forms of interaction in all aspects of society. Society and organization may be characterized as, ultimately, dependent upon the micropolitics of encounters, encounters in which meaning, interpretation, and role playing are crucial features.

If such a perspective is adopted, and we are not saying that any one of our respondents had clearly and *explicitly* adopted such a view, it has very different implications for the activities of the potential agent of change. If the organization is taken to be a political arena, then appeals to 'consensus' and to 'openness', 'trust' and even 'confrontation' may not only be taken to be partisan but also dangerous, and occasionally, counterproductive but always and inevitably as 'political'.

> In this organization, any for that matter, you live and breathe politics. Asking questions is a political act, you can't avoid it and you shouldn't.

As indicated above, no one of our respondents had an articulated framework within which they could fit their political activities. Some, while noting the incidence of manipulation, information control, imposition of definitions and the like, regretted it and wished the organization, and life, to be otherwise. For solace, and dreams of what might be, they turned to the numerous texts which advocate the truth/love model which we have outlined above. Others felt the need for an alternative framework:

> I think that links in with what I've been saying about the sixties, because I think they just totally ignore power in organizations. I've actually looked back at text books of the day, and I mean, power doesn't appear. It just does not appear. To me the social scientists of those days were ignoring it as an issue when it is, in fact, essential to me . . . .

Since the 1960s, of course, (and even in them for that matter) social scientists have become much more concerned with power and, to a lesser extent, with politics. Nonetheless, such perspectives as are available receive scant attention in the texts concerned with Organization Development. With this in mind, we feel justified in spending some pages outlining a rudimentary political framework for intervention. Our purpose in so doing is not to claim that any of our respondents operated from within the framework since it was not available to them; rather it is to erect a structure within which their experienced activities and views could not only make sense but could also appear to have some intellectual legitimacy. To regard or to have one's activities regarded as 'political' is often to be seen in a less than favourable light. The term 'political' is rarely used in anything less than a pejorative sense: by outlining a view of all social interaction as fundamentally 'political', we hope to encourage a less stigmatized reaction to the activities of us all as organization politicians.

We begin with a series of somewhat foolhardy assertions.[1] We consider nearly all behaviour to be fundamentally theatrical and political in the sense that when one individual interacts with another, more often than not the way he presents himself is motivated by that actor's need to secure some benefit from the interaction, even if that benefit may be nothing more than a reduction of uncertainty. Furthermore, we believe that the benefits of some patterns of interaction are such that those who benefit are strongly inclined to promote the *status quo* and to resist changes in those patterns.

Thus the theatrical and political aspects of life in organizations, the struggle of reasonable men to present themselves in a reasonable light and to have what they consider to be right and proper prevail, derive from the processes of human association. And in what follows we will seek to outline what we take to be the basic processes which underpin all behaviour and will consider some of the implications of these ideas for the understanding of organizational behaviour and the practice of intervention.

Our second assumption — which we will elaborate upon — is that interaction, direct face-to-face communication, constitutes the basis of all social structure. Weinstein (1969) puts the point clearly:

> If the sociologist's principal abstraction, social structure, has any concrete expression, it is to be found in myriad everyday social encounters. The operation of the larger system is dependent upon the successful functioning of the microscopic and episodic action systems generated by these encounters. And these in turn require that participants are able to effectively pursue their personal goals. In the long view, if social structure is to be stable, individuals must be successful in achieving personal purposes.

The third assumption is that organization can only be realized, that microscopic and episodic action can only occur, and that individual purposes can only be achieved through the sharing of meaning about particular events, situations, and relationships and that such sharing is realized symbolically, rhetorically, and dramatically. People in each other's presence take steps to ensure that others, party to the particular encounter or transaction, are made aware of their purposes and intentions, as they want them to be 'taken account of'. In any given interaction, social actors will take steps not only to present their own intentions and purpose but also to determine the identity and purposes of the other social actors involved. Each social actor makes the other aware and, in turn, is made aware of the other's identity and purposes by the taking of the necessary steps to publicize identities and intentions. Whatever the actor publicizes, either by dress, posture, gesture, or speech, becomes the data that the other actors can 'take account of' and thereby can 'orient' their own behaviour accordingly.

> In other words the actor becomes aware of the other's subjective 'experience' *only to the extent that these experiences are dramaturgically available*. Interaction proceeds as the basis of *whatever it is that one takes to* be the other's subjective experience . . . .
> (Perinbanayagam, 1974)

Our would-be interventionist is, of course, no different to anyone else in this process (though he may be more aware of the process than the other actors involved in it). In setting up his interventions, for example, he approaches the event with a plan of action; a sequence of behaviour he intends to initiate and which he hopes will be acceptable to his client. It may be that he wishes to have a relatively unstructured exploration or that he wishes to press ahead with a series of questions to test a particular hypothesis he is developing. Either way he must signal his intentions to his client and must take account of his reactions and his plans and dispositions. The respective plans and dispositions cannot be known until the interaction is under way and this can only be accomplished if one party seeks to indicate to the other what his intended course of action is. The potential client becomes aware of and can take account of the other's plans and intentions only to the extent that he publicizes and acts them out, and, of course, *vice versa*. Thus if the potential client declares by word and gesture that *he* wishes to control the interview, then such behaviour is presumed to indicate his desired goals; the would-be interventionist does not need to accept this pre-emptive strike but he must take it into account in constructing his own response.

At its simplest level, it can be taken that each actor begins to act in the situation in accordance with his preliminary definition of it. The behaviour is interpreted by the other actor as indicating how he, the first actor, intends to act as the encounter unfolds and is evaluated for its implications for the line of action proposed by the second actor. Thus, like dogs, the actors in the early stages of interaction may circle each other warily, seeking to sniff out the likely relationship and the course of action likely to be the most rewarding. Interaction is in essence a tentative process, a process whereby each individual is evaluating and testing the conception he has of the role and the plans of other individuals. Depending upon this interpretation and evaluation, the social actor may or may not commit himself to a particular line of action and since commitment almost always involves some risks, the ability to see situations from the standpoint of others becomes very crucial indeed. If our would-be interventionist commits himself to a line of action which profoundly disturbs the potential client and if on noting the reaction he fails to recover, he has, in effect, failed to achieve his goal with all that may mean for his anticipated project, let alone his self-esteem.

A colleague of ours provides a good illustration of the process we are seeking to outline. She wished to collect some data on decision-making processes within a particular institution (where, as it happens, she was employed). Her preferred style was to conduct relatively unstructured sessions with a number of individuals to gather their perceptions about specific decisions. One particular respondent was the head of the institution who was, she reports, somewhat disturbed at the whole notion that people's perceptions may differ and was profoundly disturbed at her lack of explicit, testable hypothesis. Part way through the interview, he interrupted her along the following lines:

> Look here, you may or may not know that I have been a Professor
> and I can tell you that this is not the way to go about doing research . . . .

She reports that throughout the rest of the interview—which thereafter did not take long—the 'interaction was somewhat stilted'. The ex-Professor answered blandly and with mounting exasperation—styles were clearly incompatible.

Not surprisingly, therefore, each social actor pays a great deal of attention to details in what are anticipated to be problematic encounters. In broad terms, the individual may know what to expect of interviews, but in the specific situation he makes use of whatever information he can in defining and interpreting the exact nature of the emergent interaction. One such source of information, the importance of which is attested in everyday life, is 'first impressions', which often consist of a hotch-potch of factors such as appearance, voice characteristics, general demeanour, sex, race, colour, and so on. We make judgements about others and are ourselves judged in terms of our dress, our accents, our bodily composure, our steadiness of gaze, our sex and our racial characteristics. We submit that we all know this and, even though we may not like it, the planning and control of appearances is part of our overall strategy for achieving our goals.

At one level or another, the respondents to our interventions were very much aware of the importance of managing impressions. Quite a number of them were concerned with their titles and their sponsoring departments. A number of them actively sought to dissociate themselves from personnel and to associate themselves with line functions or with more 'business orientated' staff departments. A number mentioned the importance of dress and posture to us and at least one external carried with him a small notebook within which he had recorded the names of his clients and facts about their families, friends and so on, with which, immediately before meeting them again, he could refresh his memory and 'appear to be very much on the ball'.

Most admitted to some kind of preparation for meetings with potential clients during which sessions they not only developed an overall strategy for the potential change programme but they also planned in some detail who was to do the talking and what issues were to be raised in what sort of sequence. For many of our respondents, as little was left to chance as possible.

> I took great pains to ensure that I was not seen to be working from a personnel base and I take just as much care in ensuring that the way I present myself does not set up any barriers. I wear a suit like the rest of them here, I read the Financial Times and I am prepared to talk about hard-headed business things. I'm here to contribute to the business success of this organization and like to be seen like that —not like somebody who is just into 'human behaviour' for the fun of it.

> I think that dress is important, I'm careful about what I wear when I go to see a client. You must not challenge their norms un-necessarily.

Our appearance is hardly a matter of chance, even in circumstances less likely to lead to conscious manipulation of it than are interviews. We choose which clothes to buy (even the decision to allow someone else to purchase for us tells us something) and we choose whether to have a haircut, whether to shave, whether to use after-shave or not and so forth. Each decision says something about how we see ourselves in everyday circumstances and situations. But we have a complicated perspective on appearance; we know that our appearance and demeanour can affect the response of others so we may contrive to dress and behave appropriately. We may appear for our meeting with a client in a dark suit and we may articulate clearly and, hopefully, cogently with a steady and direct gaze and a body posture which indicates control and influence. We may construct, that is, an appearance which will lead us to be treated how we would like to be treated. All the time, however, we are aware that appearances may be contrived and impressions may be managed and we realize that just as we may try to see through the contrivances and impressions of others, so they may be seeking to 'see through' what we are contriving. From the onset of any encounter, therefore, and continuing throughout it, each actor may be simultaneously seeking to manage the impressions he gives of himself and to see through the impressions others seek to present of themselves.

The presentation of self is thus a key feature of all interaction. It discloses who we wish to be and how we wish to be treated; it also discloses who we wish others to be and how we wish to treat them. Self-presentation, that is, casts not only our own part in the situational script, it also casts others into parts. The roles made by participants in a particular situation are reciprocal — the role of interviewee played by an individual implies the role of interviewer. The notion of presentation of self focuses upon the individual's effort to make a role and present an appearance of that role to others. Altercasting examines the other side of the coin, as it were, the effect that the process of self-presentation has upon the other party's ability to respond. Each effort at self-presentation is in a sense an attempt to constrain the potential response; if I behave as a teacher, my presentation casts you into the role of pupil; if I present myself as helpless, I seek to impose on you the role of helper. The process of altercasting operates by seeking to place limits upon the capacity of others to play parts of their own choosing. One example of this altercasting may be drawn from our dealings with the respondents to this survey. One of us wrote at the time:

> It always felt that coming away from this person, one had been sitting at the feet of a very erudite, wordy person and you always felt as though you had gone away with some homework to do, some articles you'd promised to read and more often than not, next time you went back to see this person, he checked up to see whether or not you had done your homework and if you hadn't, you got dreadfully embarrassed.

A case of very successful casting of the interviewer *in statu pupillari*.

All interventionists are conversant with this activity since they are explicitly advised to act so as to have their clients assume responsibility for the outcomes of particular exercises. At the very least, this means they are to act so as not to create dependency, not to present themselves in such a fashion that their clients have little choice but to become fawning, cringing sycophants. Some texts go further and advocate specific actions which, if successfully carried out, will cast the clients into the desired roles:

> The purpose, then, is not only to 'get the patient well'. Far more is the purpose to develop interests and skills in the client that provide him with diagnostic skills which will permit him to help judge his own interactional health, as well as that of his organization. (Golembiewski, 1972)

Such activities were also alluded to by a number of our respondents.

> It's not my job to do it for the client. It's my job to help him to do it himself.

> It's his business, not mine, I'm only there to help him sort it out for himself.

> I'm a helper and a facilitator not a doer. Doing is the client's responsibility.

> We've got to leave him better off than when we came in. We act so as to give him the skill to dispense with us.

> For the most part we seek to collaborate with them rather than work for them.

> My job was simply being a continuity person between meetings, acting as a catalyst, collecting up ideas, putting thoughts on paper for them.

> I see my role as somebody just to hold the hand of the boss while he thinks through his own problem.

> We have the right balance where he just uses me to reflect some of his ideas against me, talk about the strategy and his style—that sort of thing.

Some took the opposite point of view:

> Whatever the books say we are in the business of making the client dependent upon us.

> It's magic, isn't it? They do not know how we do it and if you

want to stay in the magic business you don't show people how you
do the tricks.

The nature of altercasting, therefore, is to impute roles to individuals and to act towards them on the basis of this imputation and thus, often very effectively, to manage their responses.

Altercasting and the presentation of self are thus two sides of the same coin: both are processes which are operative in the establishment of scripts and roles. Self-presentation not only indicates who the social actor wishes to be taken for and what he takes the interaction to be about, it also seeks to place limits on the parts to be played by others.

Each actor acts on the basis of his particular definition; as he expresses what he takes to be the appropriate behaviour it becomes obvious whether or not his perspective is shared by others. In many cases the various definitions are compatible; people are familiar with the situational script, and find few problems with the roles assigned to them and fit their lines and actions to those of others with little or no difficulty. Thus few problems arise where preliminary definitions and initial impressions are accurate predictions of the developing situation.

The degree to which this occurs is, of course, variable. Not all situations are such that we know what is expected of us and not all situations are such that, even though we know what to expect, we are willing to accept the parts assigned to us. Scripts are rendered problematic when social actors discover that their expectations are not compatible with those of other social actors party to the encounter. Such encounters not infrequently occur between change agents and particular actors within the client system. A number of our respondents reported problematic encounters between themselves and senior people in the hierarchy. In some of these encounters, the superior treated the subordinate as a more intimate friend or ally than had previously been taken to be the case. To treat someone as a privileged confidant, of course, is a well-known ploy in seeking to secure his or her cooperation in a project, their support for which is otherwise problematic. In other circumstances, the superior 'picks off' the opposition by moving in close and seeking to discover what has passed between the consultant and others in the organization. To all intents and purposes, the friendly script may be sincere and well-intentioned and not obviously invoked to elicit secrets, making it doubly difficult for the employee to perceive what, if anything, may underlie the dialogue and to take appropriate action.

Such subterfuge, if subterfuge it is, was rarely reported to us. More often than not, problems arose when the senior manager simply and openly sought information about particular individuals or particular projects, information which the interventionist knew to have been obtained in confidence. Where one party becomes aware of the role into which he or she is being cast, one of a number of options may be invoked.

First, he can decide to take no further part in the interaction. The interventionist can break off the intention abruptly or otherwise and take up some other activities. In breaking off the interaction, the actor forfeits his chance to achieve his own immediate personal goals (and, possibly in the case of the boss/subordinate example, his longer term ones as well.)

Second, the person may simply accept the scripts invoked by the other even though he is initially unwilling to do so. The interventionist tells himself that it is too much trouble and not worth the effort to oppose the boss, so even though he doesn't like it, he goes along with the script, but does so with some circumspection and a lack of commitment which he is careful not to signal too obviously. A number of our respondents took this course of action, feeding carefully selected nuggets of information to their superiors. A number of them reported going further and declared that they regularly provided information to senior members of the organization, though they did this, they said, to bring about change rather than simply to peddle gossip.

Thirdly, and very unusually, the actor may draw attention to the nature of the interaction itself and seek explicitly to renegotiate it. Thus the interventionist may declare that his boss's actions are putting him in an untenable position *vis-à-vis* his clients and that this is not a role he wishes to be assigned. Such an option implies an ability to recognize explicitly what is going on and, more importantly, a personal style which enables the actor to draw attention to it in a manner which does not produce denial and defensiveness. From our evidence, we would consider that such abilities and inclinations are in short supply though, again, a number of our respondents appeared to be able to manage this quite successfully.

The fourth option is much more frequently observed. The actor in rejecting the part assigned for him and denying the situational script which has been proposed simply seeks to impose his own definition upon the other actor. If he has decided either to call off the interaction or to accept the initial definitions of the other actor, the result will be clear. If not, if he has decided to escalate the competition, as it were, by imposing his own definition of the situation, the result will be much less clear. Each actor thus declares himself to be interested in pursuing the interaction, but on his own terms. The outcome is likely to be a compromise definition minimally acceptable to each of the actors but not preferred by either. In the case of the boss/employee relationship, for example, the boss may prefer to reduce the interpersonal differences between himself and his subordinate to the point at which he can 'pump' him about specific projects and individuals. The employee may prefer to keep his distance and to define the relationship in purely task terms, feeding him information on a limited scale. Much of the interaction will be concerned with the boss expressing his view and the employee his and may proceed *temporarily* on the basis of, say, conversation about relationships elsewhere in the organization.

We emphasise the word 'temporarily' since the working agreement is problematic in its attainment and far from stable; it is a delicate balance of interactive processes and is easily upset. That it is likely to be upset is evident when we consider the preferred goals of those party to it; one wishes to push in one direction, one wishes to push in the other. If the working agreement is upset, it is neither the end of the world nor necessarily will it result in the termination of the encounter. A new one will be reached, which in turn may be upset and superseded. 'A single encounter, then, often presents the appearance of successive phases of interaction, each marketed by the negotiation of a new working agreement' (McCall and Simmons, 1966).

As with the boss, so with the client. Relations between interventionist and client may be characterized as passing through a number of 'working agreements', each in turn a reflection of the salient and occasionally idiosyncratic dispositions and plans of those party to them (Mangham, 1979).

> I like to start off pretty low profile with my clients. I negotiate a role for myself with them of sitting back and observing but that doesn't often last long. Sooner or later they put pressure on me to participate and our relationship develops from there.

> It's often quite sticky to start off with, you being a stranger to them and that, but after a while, particularly if you can say something that pulls people up short, or make a presentation of a set of ideas which they really latch on to, it becomes a lot more fluid and relaxed. You are accepted as part of the group.

> It's often difficult terminating a relationship with a set of people you have spent a lot of time with. Can be a bit messy. Sometimes I must stop going to the meetings, at other times I negotiate a finish and leave more gracefully.

> Some of the groups want a lot from you, some a little; some seem to want you there just to kick you now and again. Can be a very odd kind of relationship really.

> Once I've isolated a situation, I note who is involved and make my own judgements about who are the key people to see; I then visit them on a one-off basis and my aim would be usually to get them to sit down together in a room somewhere and say, 'this may or may not be true, but I suspect that we've got a problem here, can I ask whether you think we've got a problem?' Usually, if I've done my homework properly, they would say, 'I guess you've got a point and this is something we must do'. Then we go to some kind of strategic planning phase—very simple, just two or three key things —to make not a miracle but a kind of margin of improvement.

> It's usually a bit dodgy to start off with. I'm not sure of them; they are not sure of me, nor—in some cases—of each other. As we come to grips with issues that matter to them and as I am seen to be of some help in this, relations change. They change again when they come to recognize I'm virtually steering the ship for them and

end up happy to see me leave. You can see that when you first meet them, they can't so it's all a bit strange . . . .

And so each actor approaches an encounter with a preliminary definition of what may happen and what part he is willing to play in it and what part he expects others to play. At the onset of the interaction he must take into account the behaviour of others including their attempts to constrain or channel his own behaviour. Often the preliminary definitions of the individuals coincide and each person is able to proceed with his original plans with the full cooperation of other individuals. Occasionally, definitions are incompatible and a process of negotiation occurs, influenced by the physical setting, the props and appliances of others, as well as by their specific rewards and sanctions and the anticipated responses of others not even necessarily physically present. The outcome is a temporary agreement, a negotiated reality which allows the interaction to proceed on at least a temporary basis. What usually transpires in problematic situations is that individuals are seldom allowed to perform exactly the role they would like nor do they comply exactly with the roles which they are cast by others.

Continuation of the interaction is dependent, therefore, on the ability of the participants to accommodate or at least to align themselves with part of the projected and interpreted reality. What develops, in effect, is an agreement not to disagree; a working agreement that allows the participants to proceed, characterized not by consensus and clear agreement, but more by the absence of large scale disagreement. At the very centre of human behaviour, potentially therefore, is struggle and resolution, negotiation, process, and flux.

Now a number of conclusions may be drawn from this; first, and perhaps most fundamentally for the approach taken here, all situations, even the most routine and least problematic, are created and sustained by the interpretations and actions of those involved. Even the most boring and predictable situational script is dependent upon and is only kept going by its members, and may, within limits, be changed by those members. Second, and clearly related to the foregoing, individuals inhabit a reality which they create and then respond to as if it were an entity, a thing which stands apart from and beyond them. Social order in organizations and elsewhere cannot be sustained without the active support and commitment of individuals. Organization can be viewed as a complex network of interactions involving, at their very core, interpreting and acting individuals. Thus organization may be conceived of as a process of creating, maintaining, and, occasionally, dissolving relationships and the organization, at any one time, may be seen as a network of such joint actions.

Put another way, organization may be seen as a process—a continuous exchange of definitions and affirmation or otherwise of working agreements— and not simply as a structure of rules, regulations and procedure within which all is order. All shared understandings lack permanence and must be continually reaffirmed or renegotiated; rules, procedures, order, and structure are not automatic occurrences (however taken for granted they may appear) but rather must be worked at and sustained by the repeated acts of participants. The working agreements which characterize organizational life arise from and are dependent upon the processes of give and take, diplomacy, imposition, and bargaining. Order and change may thus be seen as the products of negotiation, the result of the pulling and hauling that constitute the political bargaining process which occurs between individuals and groups as they struggle to achieve *their* goals and objectives in association with or at the expense of others.[2]

Now, whatever else it is and however much remains to be worked out or substantiated, such a perspective on behaviour is in marked contrast to that usually available to the potential interventionist. The 'classic' volumes referred to elsewhere in this book tend to be short on power and politics and long on systems, truth, and love; by and large they ignore that which Burke (1974) refers to as the 'darker side of humanity'. If, however, behaviour is conceptualized along the lines developed above and elsewhere (Allison, 1971; Mangham, 1978, 1979) then it may be reasonable to consider consulting and intervening in similar terms. The image of the consultant as eunuch or friendly neighbourhood helper may, in any case, need some reappraisal. Perhaps many, if not all, who adopt the role of consultant or interventionist do so from a desire to change the world: to reduce oppression, stimulate human dignity, release human energy, increase productivity, what you will. It does not much matter what — what matters is that each of us has an interest; each of us is working towards some end; each of us presents himself and seeks to control others so as to validate that set of goals and that self-image. In this sense even the behaviour of a saint is deeply selfish and fundamentally political. Few interventionists would claim to be saints, though, as noted in the previous chapter, many are treated as gurus and some have the reputation of being able to walk on water.

If the framework outlined above has any utility it is in alerting us to the fact that no intervention, process or otherwise, is neutral. A decision to draw attention to the process of a meeting has implications for the behaviour and the relationships of those involved; it is an attempt to draw attention to the rules and thus to disrupt 'working agreements'. It is, in essence, a political act and can be nothing else and thus had better be approached with some degree of circumspection and framed so as to achieve some degree of support. Similarly, if more obviously, a recommendation that a re-organization take place or a reporting relationship be changed is clearly a political act however much the consultant may take refuge behind his or her technical diagnosis.

A number of our respondents were very clear about their responsibilities in this respect:

This Personnel Management Guide is a key document for me because in the writing of it I'm going to make some statements that I personally believe and I'm not quite sure how many others do;

and so I'm going to have to fight through the normal bureaucratic channels before it will see the light of day and get published. And it may have to be modified. Since I'm a tactician and a politician, I'll accept some modifications in the greater interests of getting the thing out - getting 70 per cent of my stuff on the table.

It's all a question of power, really, and, by definition, playing political games — trying to get something done that you believe in — can be dangerous. If you play with fire you occasionally get burned.

The lesson is to watch power, implicit power. The power thing is both a healthy thing and a disabling thing and you've got to choose.

I'm developing ideas which are a threat to their (managers') status, their position, their authority, their responsibilities. They won't like it, that's a fact of life, and if you don't see it as a fact of life you are just putting your head in the sand.

It's very important to only do something disturbing if the organization is ready to cope with the consequences. It is counter-productive when they're not ready.

You've got to become more and more prescriptive and violate expectations deliberately, but not too much, or you spatter them against the wall and that's when they say, that's when I mean you are thrown out; that's failure, and if you are completely absorbed by the organization, that's failure too.

The answer, for my money, is to get at the key control systems and start to work there. That's where the OD starts. And that's where you have to face tough problems because you're dealing with reactionary elements in the organization, but they've got to be faced or risk an explosion later on.

You need to find out who the levers are and you *have* to work with them.

Once you are into the game of power . . . there's the inevitability of conflict.

Just another case where the boss was dragging his feet and I chatted with the director concerned and he squeezed the boss and by that fact we were able to change it.

We have tried in this chapter to present and illustrate a framework which (like that of Thompson, 1967) represents organizations as political arenas within which different people and individuals struggle to promote their own interests.[3] A number of interesting studies, notably by Pettigrew, have looked at the role of specialist groups such as OD people within the political process, but our emphasis has been exclusively individual since our respondents talked about themselves as solo operators. Although many belonged to groups and mentioned other individuals as colleagues, none talked about departmental or group politics. The emphasis throughout was upon individual survival and individual achievement.

> It's all about me in the final analysis. I suppose it's a kind of existential trip. Me versus the rest and I succeed in the end.

> I work very much alone and I prefer it that way.

> I'm a team of one and nearly always operate as a loner.

The framework may or may not be useful in illustrating the nature of the relations between consultant and client and, at a more general level, in depicting the broad sweep of organizational life. We believe that it helps to make sense of a number of activities that we have observed, that have been reported to us and that we have ourselves indulged in. At least as presented here it has a number of weaknesses: a strong emphasis upon relations between individuals (and much of intervention is at this level) but a corresponding under-emphasis upon the systemic properties of organizations; an open acknowledgement of the importance of power but no real exploration of the factors which may or may not affect the ability of one actor or group of actors to impose their definitions upon others (Mangham, 1979). By far the largest omission is any discussion of values. As we have seen, the classic writers were strong on values, a strength which is emphasized in notions such as organizational health and organizational effectiveness, which are usually associated with the quality of interpersonal relations. The notion of effectiveness was occasionally mentioned by our 'political' respondents but rarely in a systematic or thought through fashion. Few if any of our respondents were able to articulate what they took to be the desired and desirable outcome of their efforts; compared to notions dear to those interventionists in the classic mould such as enhancing relationships and accelerating self-actualization, much of what our respondents have to say about what it is they are up to is thin gruel indeed hardly enough to sustain vigorous souls. It is worth noting, however, that they are not alone in their inability to specify with some degree of concreteness what they mean by effectiveness. A recent book by Goodman and Pennings (1977) states unequivocally that 'effectiveness is one of the most pervasive yet least delineated organizational constructs'—a theme which is taken up again and again by the book's panel of distinguished contributors.

Values, other than those which are thought to enhance effectiveness, are an equally fuzzy area for our respondents. As we have seen, those in the classic mould can produce a list as long as your arm. A number are implied in our sample of views derived from 'politicians' but nowhere are they explicitly stated. There appeared to be an emphasis upon expertise, or implicit apprecia-tion of professionalism which occasionally took the form of 'I know what's good for my client'. Sometimes this was more openly espoused (some may say 'arrogantly asserted'): 'they don't appreciate what I'm driving at but in a few years' time they will understand . . . .

An equally strong, but equally implicit, value appeared to be attached to manipulation. A number of our respondents appeared to epitomize the old Italian proverb: 'Never do today the thing you can get someone else to do for you tomorrow.' One or two of our respondents openly prided themselves on their ability to manipulate others.

> How does anyone influence anyone? Some people can do it — I'm
> not saying I'm so good at it but, you know, let's just say I work at
> it.

Some revelled in their position of eminence grise, sitting at the centre of the event, waiting, watching, and pouncing as appeared appropriate:

> You could say I sit at the centre of a whole web of information,
> watching and waiting for the opportunity to use it.

> If I'm right, most of what people need is someone like me pressing
> on the conscience.

A related idea was the value that many placed upon the idea of seeding, keeping a 'low profile' but setting out to influence by dropping ideas here, there and everywhere and carefully nurturing them until they were healthy enough to be fully exploited. Others took themselves to be less manipulative but placed a considerable emphasis upon notions such as 'readiness' and 'appropriate interventions' which, in effect, left a great deal of often unexamined powers and influence in the hands of themselves.

In conclusion we can point to the stark (if somewhat artificial) contrast between what we take to be classic approaches and the 'political' one adopted by a number of our respondents. The classics are primarily — not exclusively — interested in the development of individuals; they are for truth, openness, choice, mutuality, responsibility, and valid information. They tend to know where they are going even if their activities seem out of place in what others take to be the rough and tumble of organizations. They are clearly on the side of the angels in that they are working for more 'human' organizations. The politics, in contrast, are less sure that they are for truth and openness unless being for it produces some desired movement in the organization; in other words, for them at least, truth and openness are means not ends. They are sensitive to power and influence and tend to be tuned in to the networks and appear to be much more skilled at riding the corporate tiger than their classic counterparts. The question as to what end their activities are directed remains, however, naggingly open.

We wish to conclude by referring to the common response to much of the foregoing; in our experience, it is listened to either with mounting irritation or a kind of 'Thank-god-someone-has-said-it-at-last' expression of relief. Those irritated declare us *personae non gratae*; such views, they assert, are untenable in this fraternity, political behaviour on the part of consultants does not constitute organization development. Such an assertion comes from those who work within the normative framework of a 'humanistic' set of values and is, of course, tenable, indeed mandatory, within such a framework. Similar comments may also be made by skilled politicos who do not wish to have their cover blown. The other comment, the expression of relief, comes from those who have been trapped, as it were, by the humanistic views which they take to have stifled organizational development. Many consultants and interventionists work within systems marked by non-humanistic values, assumptions and processes and are effectively paralysed by the circumstances in which they find themselves. Emotionally and dispositionally not inclined to become consciously involved in the political process, they can do little but bewail the system or draw up more grandiose schemes for effecting attitude changes; schemes which they lack the stomach for forcing through. Indeed the notion of pushing and pulling appears to run counter to cherished notions such as choice and consensus. For a number of other people, the idea that effecting change itself is a political process, that it is not 'wrong' to struggle, to fix, to manipulate, and to manoeuvre in the service of one's goals, is positively invigorating and warmly welcomed.

For such people, we will finish with a marginally reassuring quote from Kelman who discusses the ethical dilemma we all face in our work. The dilemma has two dimensions. Many of us hold the enhancement of man's freedom of choice as a fundamental value and its follows that any deliberate influencing of the behaviour of others constitutes a violation of that value. On the other hand, effective behaviour change involves some degree of utilization of power and control and a potential imposition of our ideas and our values. According to Kelman, however, and worth thinking about . . . 'there exists no formula for so structuring an effective change situation that such manipulation is totally absent'. It may all be a matter of degree but we would suggest that political behaviour, as defined here, is part and parcel of every instance of successful planned change.

Notes

1. Much of what follows derives from Mangham (1978, 1979) which, in turn owes much to Allison (1971), Göffman (1959), Blumer (1969) and numerous others.
2. Clearly there are all kinds of qualifications and additions to be made to what we have said so far—negotiated order is affected by factors such as power (of superior, colleague, and subordinate), socialization, communication, personal factors such as

the 'need' for inclusion, affection, and control. We have treated such factors elsewhere (Mangham, 1979).
3. For a more sophisticated framework along similar lines see Goodman and Pennings (1977).

References

Allison, G. T. (1971). *Essence of Decision*, Boston: Little Brown.
Blumer, H. (1969). *Symbolic Interactionism*, Englewood Cliffs, NJ: Prentice-Hall.
Burke, W. W. (1974). Organization Development in transition. *Journal of Applied Behavioural Science*, **12**, 22–43.
Cyert, R. M., and March, J. G. (1959). *A Behavioural Theory of the Firm*. Englewood Cliffs, NJ: Prentice-Hall.
Goffman, E. (1959). *The Presentation of Self in Everyday Life*, Garden City, New York: Doubleday.
Golembiewski, R. (1972). *Renewing Organizations*, Itasca, Illinois: F. E. Peacock.
Goodman, P. S., and Pennings, J. M. (eds.) (1977). *New Perspectives on Organizational Effectiveness*, San Francisco: Jossey Bass.
McCall, G. J., and Simmons, J. L. (1966). *Identities and Interactions*, New York: Free Press.
Mangham, I. L. (1978). *Interactions and Interventions in Organizations*, Chichester: John Wiley and Sons.
Mangham, I. L. (1979). *The Politics of Organizational Change*, London: Associated Business Press.
Perinbanayagam, R. S. (1974). The definition of the situation: an analysis of the ethnomethodological and dramaturgical view. *Sociological Quarterly*, **15**, 521–541.
Thompson, J. D. (1967). *Organizations in Action*, McGraw-Hill, New York.
Weinstein, E. A. (1969). The Development of Interpersonal Competence in Goslin, P. (Ed.), *Handbook of Socialization Theory and Research*, Chicago, Illinois: Rand McNally.

Chapter 5

The Genesis of Interventions

Where do Interventions Come From?

A central concept throughout this book has been that of 'intervention'. An intervention takes place when someone works on an organization in a way that is intended not only to affect some state or event within that organization, but also, so to change beliefs, feelings, relationships, processes, and suchlike within that organization, that future change is in some way facilitated.

If we study interventions, however, only from the point when they are in full flow, we miss a lot of questions about the conception, gestation and birth of an intervention which might be valuable for us to consider. How does it come about that someone is invited in to an organization to intervene in it? Who decides (and how) that an intervention is desirable? How is a particular interventionist chosen? How is a decision reached as to what shall be the focus of the intervention, and what shall be the central issue or issues that should be addressed within it? How do particular persons make themselves heard over their chosen view of what an intervention should be about? Who decides (and how) which of the parties involved should be regarded as the primary clients of the intervention?

In posing these questions, we are addressing a different area of discourse from the one which has been the focus of most of the existing Organization Development literature, as reflected in the bibliography at the end of this book. There, writers have predominantly addressed questions of style and effectiveness in bringing about change, such as, 'How can consultants best respond when someone comes to talk to them about an issue?' 'What can consultants most effectively set about doing from that point?'

Our analysis of what different people connected with interventions think they are doing before, during, and after the point at which a consultant is invited in, raises a more fundamental question: irrespective of questions of skills and effectiveness in introducing organizational change, how does some person or group decide that they want some sort of organizational change, and how do they decide what sort it is that they want? The answers to these questions have relevance for the discussion of effective consulting action, but the questions that we shall be discussing are ones that are not even asked if the issues are defined in terms of traditional Organization Development terminology.

In this chapter, we shall look first at the relationship between interventions and issues, that is, between interventions and whatever it is in a person's organizational world that makes them want an intervention. To prevent it causing too many problems later, we look at this point at the relationship between issues and problems. Then we shall consider the way that issues for intervention seemed to be 'made not born', according to the accounts of our interviewees. After that we go on to look at how issues for intervention may be constructed and reconstructed, and at some practical considerations in doing this; thus issues are seen as going on from being 'made' to a process of remaking and reconstructing. This leads us to consider issue finding (or 'making') as a negotiative process embedded in organizational politics, and then to some special features of the consultant role in this negotiation. Partly because of these special features, a relationship emerged in the research between consultants and issues, and that is the subject of the next section. As well as reconstructing an issue out of a situation, it seems that issues may be displaced by surrogate issues; the two concepts are different because the surrogate issue is only a replacement with respect to the mental processes of the person for whom it displaces the issue, whilst a reconstructed issue relates both to those processes and to the situation from which the issue was constructed. Finally, we draw together these arguments and suggest that considering where interventions come from may lead us to think differently about our interventions and hence to take different actions.

Interventions and Issues

We find it convenient to talk about interventions as being concerned with issues, where an issue is some matter which is of interest or concern to the person or persons for whom it is an issue. Thus when we speak of issues this does not necessarily imply that there is a 'problem' in the sense of something being deficient or having gone wrong in the organization or part of an organization in which an intervention is wanted. What we do mean is that there is some central question, point, or phrase which is used as a way of defining what the intervention is about. Thus, for example, some interventions are labelled as being about 'team building', 'participation', 'improving communications', 'role negotiation', 'stress', 'personal growth', and so on. It may be implied that there is something wrong which the intervention is meant to put right, but equally an intervention with any of these labels may be intended to improve something without any implication of culpable deficiency.

In our research we have been trying to discover how a particular issue comes to be regarded as central to an intervention. We are not suggesting that such issues are 'problems', except in the limited sense that they are situations where someone wishes something to be other than it is. If this were not so, they would not want an intervention. One apparent exception to this arose during our research, and that is the case where persons believe that an intervention may have a conservative effect, whether or not that is their intention. Thus one consultant told us about how repeated reorganizations in his company had the effect of maintaining the *status quo*:

> Plus ça change — everything changes, nothing changes.

Even this does not strictly conflict with our contention that interventions are essentially about issues, because it depends on one of the confusions which surround the word 'change'. Even a deliberately conservative intervention is intended to make changes, in the sense that those changes are to prevent change that would otherwise have occurred, 'all other things being equal'.

If interventions are defined by issues, then to know about where interventions come from we need to know how the issues which define further in to this, which is the next phase of our argument, we shall spend a little more time on the question of issues and problems.

Issues and Problems

We have said that the issues which are used to define interventions are not necessarily problems in the sense of there being a deficiency of something. The languages of organization development and of problem solving are so soft at this point (that is, there is so little consensus about the meaning of words) that it is very difficult to ask consultants questions that make sense about where issues or problems come from. Misunderstandings can easily arise, as with the consultant whom we were trying to ask about whether the problem which underlay a particular intervention had come from him or from his clients, and who answered:

> I don't think it's a problem-solving project, and I'm very suspicious now of problem-solving projects. It's a developmental project.

This made us more careful in future to explain that our object was to find what it was that drove the direction of a project; we were not intending to imply that there were some 'problems' needing to be solved in the narrow sense of deficiencies. While this is clearly a difficulty to do with language, the concept that we were wanting to use is so elastic in several different directions that it would be difficult to know what words could be used to overcome the difficulty. The size of the issues in terms of which people describe their interventions, for example, can vary enormously. One one hand, many consultants insist on defining tight boundaries for interventions, with limited issues, while on the other hand there was the consultant who likened his intervention to the building of cathedrals, saying:

I believe it's like some works of art, some of these magnificent cathedrals, I think it takes more than your lifetime, like your efforts live on if they're worth it, and make an impact afterwards and some other beggar sees it. It's more like the artist who's appreciated afterwards.

As well as issues for intervention being defined in different sizes, the precision and detail that is wanted in the definition itself may vary. Not everyone wants to produce a comprehensive and precise definition of every issue that they are connected with. One consultant explained a very broad piece of issue-finding in the following words:

We didn't want to get into detail. We thought that would be quite inappropriate at that stage of the work. We simply wanted to get the broad lines of concern and the broad lines of balance of the thing, so we were really testing the strength of the winds, and seeing if they were all going in the same direction, and—surprise, surprise —they weren't.

In addition to the variations in scale and precision of issue constructing, there is a variation in the urgency with which the persons whose issues they are think they should be treated. This can vary so much with different issues that it seems difficult to use the word 'issue' for all of them. The urgency with which an issue is constructed depends not only on the person's view of the urgency of the external factors relating to the issue and the speed with which inaction could lead to costs or loss of opportunity; urgency also depends on many factors within the person, such as, does he have other issues current at the moment? If so, he is less likely to construe a new issue as urgent. Does he know what to do with the new issue? If not, he may well think of it as less urgent than he would if he did know what to do with it. One consultant, for example, described an issue that he was dealing with as a puzzle, saying:

It's not consistent, it doesn't shine out that this needs doing or that needs doing. And like all puzzles, they get to the second place in your box, instead of being on top of the box, at least the puzzles that you can't work out what to do with.

We have noted a massive variation in the usage of words like 'issue' and 'problem', and suggest that this is serious, not only for those who do research on the topic. Of the various different connotations to do with the notion of 'issue' that we have discussed in this section, on the whole, no one person emphasized more than one of these connotations at any one time. Where the language is so inadequate, the resulting complexity and ambiguity both in thinking and in communicating makes it very difficult for any one to comprehend, let alone talk about, more than one of these connotations at a time, and yet it seems likely that all parties are losing from only being able to make use of a small part of the potentially available repertoire of terms and constructs of the subject.

Issues are Made, not Born

On the basis of previous research that we have conducted on problems and issues (Sims, 1978, 1979) we tend to view issues not as things that exist, and which everyone could agree about if only they had all the facts, but as ways in which an individual understands his situation. Thus if someone were to say that the issue was 'the development of my staff', we would not take him to be making an objective statement about the state of development of his staff, but rather to be making what might be a quite idiosyncratic statement about his understanding of his world. He would probably not expect that, if someone else were to take over his job the following day, the issue they were concerned with would be the same one. Thus we conceive of issues as having to do with a person trying to make his *own* sense of the world that he lives in, making sense of it not only for himself but also in a way which enables him to negotiate about that world with other persons (Mangham, 1977), and finding a way of understanding his world in terms of there being an issue in it. Thus issues are defined by persons in order to make sense of their worlds.

It seemed that several people experienced a state in which they knew they had a problem, but could not yet tell what it was. For example, one person said:

> We had meetings to talk about what was wrong. Everything wasn't right — so what was wrong?

Another person described something similar at a more personal level:

> I realized that I had got a problem, but I didn't know what it was.

In some cases people never did come to a conscious conclusion over what a problem was about. We mentioned earlier the consultant who used the metaphor of building a cathedral to talk about people thinking and working through issues. He went on to explain that sometimes he could work satisfactorily with a client without the client ever being conscious of what issue was being worked with until the particular intervention is over anyhow, and someone else passes comment on the change that has taken place.

> A year later someone says 'My God, you're so much different in that respect' . . . . That's what I'm doing, fundamentally, helping them to build their own cathedral, and they probably don't even recognize it for many many years.

Acknowledging that there is an issue, then, need not imply that you know what the issue is, nor that its nature needs to be brought to full consciousness, nor that the person is experiencing a single, unchanging issue as opposed to a 'mess' (Ackoff, 1974) of issues. Even when an issue does become conscious for a person, and they describe what the issue is, that issue may still come out differently according to various factors. For one thing, different people see different issues even in what, to an observer, is the same situation. One person, talking about repeating in another part of his organization an exercise that he had done in one part, said:

> I think we will get different types of issues emerge from the people, because the people are different and their attitude to work is different.

One of the roots of such differences which this person saw was organizational level. He said 'Different levels, different views'. Issues do not only vary because of the different natures or interests of the persons for whom they are issues. The relative power positions of the persons concerned also affect the issues that are defined. For example, we suspect that the kind of issues raised by his clients was powerfully affected by the personal style of the consultant who said:

> We'll need to watch them to make sure that they manage the whole thing in a responsible way, and the less powerful members begin to identify their real concerns.

On other occasions, variations in the issues that are defined are attributed less to personality and personal power differences, and more to such qualities as specialism in role or knowledge. One consultant told us how specialists in different fields were needed in order to define issues in those fields:

> Guys at the top are often functionally blinkered, they're not equipped with the Management of Change, the Management of Innovation, the Predictive, the Scanning, the Open Systems, all that sort of conceptual stuff with its technologies and so on. They miss out lots of dope on what we would call 'domains' in their scanning and their diagnosis.

The notion this consultant uses of 'functional blinkers' sounds similar to Merton's (1947) notion of 'trained incapacity', whereby the development of a capacity to see and understand things within the framework of some specialism implies a lower propensity and competence to see and understand outside that framework.

Different procedures for looking at issues could affect the issues which were eventually defined. In the following example a consultant told us that a particular method of diagnosis and intervention was appropriate to a company in which he was applying it, because it handled and highlighted the things that he regarded as important there. He said:

> Organizational Analysis is appropriate because it tends to throw up the environmental forces affecting the company; it would show what had been the effects on the company of the takeover.

Such comments highlight the importance of the devices that are used for finding issues. Many people believe that they operate some device which enables them to be particularly good at listening to, and finding issues from, their clients. For example:

> We'll start really with 'Where are we going?' and then put in a session round, and 'What does the past tell us about that?'; and then think about the selection process, then the communication process and the decision making process, if you like, how was one going to manage that in a fair way?

Another person described a favourite device that he used as:

> Acting very much as a sounding board, not a decision maker but simply someone who can say 'look, are you sure you know what you are talking about and do you realize you're actually saying different things', or whatever.

Issues can have a disconcerting way of moving round, it seems. In some cases this may be because a diagnosis was used which was never found convincing by the persons whose problem it was supposed to be, but in other cases it may be that a new issue is produced as a result of consultant activity. Someone told us about one case which illustrated his general belief that resolving some issues will strengthen people's wish to see yet more issues resolved:

> Once you start to sow the seed along there, you will find that the people who were quite happy, because they saw it was the same pattern of behaviour throughout the place, will cease to be happy. Why should they be treated any different to anybody else in the organization: The appetite heightens with the feeding.

As well as how issues are made, it seems to be important to some people to consider how issues are sold, or how people persuade one another of the significance of issues. One person described the beginning of a successful intervention in a group by saying that what the group liked was that:

I seemed to have got hold of one or two of the key issues in the organization very quickly, which said to them, well perhaps if he can see them that quickly, they must be there.

In this case, the consultant, by expressing some issues which seemed to resonate with the clients, gave the clients confidence both in himself and in those issues. At the same time, of course, he took a risk in that the issues he expressed might have been rejected, and that leads us on to consider the ways in which the issues around which interventions take place are made and then altered to fit circumstances.

Issues are Constructed and Reconstructed

When an issue for intervention has been named, that is not the end of the story. If a person decided to regard some particular circumstances as being an issue around which he would like to see an intervention take place, in most organization situations he will then have to persuade others that this should be regarded as an issue, without it making him look foolish ('nonsense—you don't understand') or inadequate ('can't you keep your own house in order?'). He may do this by seeking to persuade others that this issue is an issue for them too, or that it connects with an issue for them too, or that it connects with an issue for them, or he may do it by varying the issue until he finds something which he believes would make an acceptable and reasonable public issue for him. He, or someone else, would subsequently present the issue to a consultant, if an intervention was to take place, and again the person presenting the issue would pay particular attention to the impression he was making, to aspects of confidentiality, and to factors which it was felt undesirable to lay open to the consultant. Given such a chain of events, it would not be surprising if the problem which the consultant grasped and designed strategies to solve was very different from the one originally experienced. In this section we look at some of the many descriptions of how issues undergo construction and reconstruction which were given to us by those to whom we talked.

A quite frequent example of problem reconstruction was where an interventionist sought to redefine an issue in such a way that it changed from being an individual issue to being a group issue. A case of this was given to us by one consultant, who said:

> The bloke on the shop floor might feel that 'I don't want to use an intermediary', but yet the issue that he's got may be one that needs to be raised by an intermediary because it's not an individual issue but a group issue.

We did not discover how the competing definitions which the consultant is talking about were resolved in this case.

Although persons tend to see and describe themselves as reconstructing issues, they do not seem to reckon that others about them might be doing the same thing. Our data do not tell us whether this is because the people we talked to — those explicitly involved in organizational change — are more likely to be involved in issue reconstruction activities than are the rest of the organizational population, or whether it is because often people do not think of others as having as sophisticated and developed a frame of reference and action as their own. In either case, the accounts that were given show a belief that some individuals can influence reconstruction activities very strongly. We noted in particular four different attitudes that consultants seemed to take to this influence. First, there were those who believed in making full use of their influence without too much display of force. Thus one person told us about how he had run a meeting in which he had persuaded a team he was working with to think through various issues that he regarded as important, and the next stage was that 'within about a fortnight of that meeting we had worked out for them what order they would tackle the issues in'. In this case the consultant was allowing a brief burst of team activity, while keeping the structuring of the issues very much to himself. The confidence that consultants have in being able to control and define the issues in an intervention is often very great. As one of them said:

> If they do go along a path which we think is wrong, well we can change it later. It's more important that they're actually doing something, and taking initiatives, and trying to move the thing to the next step.

Secondly, there were those who used their influence to encourage their clients to engage in issue reconstruction, but who tried not to influence the direction taken in that reconstruction. This is more of a peppering approach, of trying things out till something works, and is described in the following quotation:

> What I was hoping was that by talking to them I would dig out some issues and be able to use these issues in some catalytic way, by playing them back to the organization.

Thirdly, there were the consultants who regarded the extent to which they, as influential persons, could bring about issue reconstruction as being a problem for them; even if they were trying not to influence excessively the issues of their clients, their positions of power could make it difficult not to do so, particularly if issues were only vaguely perceived by organization members. One consultant said:

> I find I have to be very careful not to suggest the things that I value very highly like team-building, like inter-personal skills, like

intergroup skills, all sorts of things of that sort, because they're normally low on security, and they'll take it and buy it, and you've got a contract for a climate survey, for £30,000 just when they don't need it.

Fourthly, a problem for some interventionists was to increase the power and influence that they could exercise over issue construction. Often they wanted to do this in order subsequently to bring about greater participation in the making of issues. For example, one person said:

We're actually quite concerned that we don't have a mechanism in the company for really getting everybody to ask, and keep on holding in focus, central questions about the objectives and the function of the company.

Some Practical Considerations about Problem Reconstruction

Organizations are all different, and many of the different practical questions raised by the consultants and clients whom we interviewed seemed to some extent peculiar to their own organizations. However, a few seemed to crop up several times. One example was summarized in the following quotation from a person describing how the use of consultative machinery could degenerate in terms of the issues produced. He said:

I've been involved in joint consultation over the years, and I've seen consultation sort of dissolve from grandiose ideas to what I call cold chip syndromes. You know, in the end that's all that's talked about, cold canteen food, cold chips.

Several of the consultants and clients we interviewed told us that reconstruction of issues could be quite hard work. One person told us that a particular issue had come through in 'rumbles' over several years, but that it wasn't until, for quite different reasons, he and a study team had to consider one of these rumbles, that the issue started emerging for them. Another person differentiated between tactical and strategic levels of issue reconstruction. He explained that he had kept on for years about a particular issue that he had wanted taken up in his organization, sending the ideas up the hierarchy in the hope that some time they would begin to reappear. They did, and when we asked him whether the idea that came back from the long journey round the organization was still recognizably the same idea, he said:

Recognizable to me, in a different form, but perhaps not recognizable to the people I had been bombarding over a period of time. It's recognizable to me, you know, it still fits within the strategic pattern of doing something within a particular field . . . .

It still meets some of the objectives that I have sought to achieve.

This consultant was working with a very sophisticated and complicated model of how the issues for intervention are reconstructed in an organization. It was unusual in that he reckoned with other people's constructions and he tried to plan his own constructions in such a way that they took account of those other constructions and were not changed in terms of their strategic effect in the process of reconstruction and political activity through which they had to go.

Perhaps the most significant practical consideration in problem construction to emerge in the research, however, was the organizational politics involved, and it is to this that we now turn.

Issue Construction is a Political, Negotiative Process

We have spoken in the last chapter of the political activities of change agents, and of the way in which we see many of the activities of persons in organizations as being political. The process of defining the issues which in turn define interventions is also political, in the sense that it is not carried out with openness, honesty, and clarity, but with much more political, covert, and instrumental norms of procedure. Consensus and collaboration are not valued particularly for their own sakes, but only sometimes as a means whereby the person can encourage issues to be found which lead to interventions of the sort that he would wish.

In some cases, this means that a powerful person simply tells subordinates to encourage or permit an intervention around a particular issue. In one case, a consultant was explaining to us how a particular intervention had started, and that the issue for intervention had not been defined by any of the management at the plant where the intervention was to take place.

> So the managing director was told that it was going to happen, and that he and the personnel manager had to negotiate with us what was going to happen.

Some of our interviewees explained this to us as a fact of organizational life, that some individuals do not even have to negotiate the definition of issues. One man, explaining how he got an intervention he wanted, said:

> I have allies in different parts . . . . There are only a few people who have a great deal of influence and power. The chairman says something casually, and it becomes policy. That is how things happen.

As well as their power to command the defining of issues, powerful individuals may also be needed to license the defining of issues. For example, one consultant told us that while it would be a good thing if a particular group defined a certain issue: 'I think it's more important for me to see the managing director outside that meeting and tell him that it's a good thing to do', nothing would be achieved if the issue that he wanted to see taken up was agreed by the persons involved but not licensed by their managing director. Licences for organizational action may be sought not from an individual but from a hierarchy.

> You see it is a complex organization — you don't make moves until you've cleared it all the way up.

In the two examples we have given of the licensing of issues by powerful persons, speaking to the licensor seemed to be a relatively straightforward process. The next two examples involve politicking in the more normal sense, where messages are being passed between persons with great care and consideration being given to the consequences of passing the messages, and to changes in the messages. In the first case the consultant finds himself in circumstances where he cannot confirm the licensing of an issue with the boss explicitly, but gives reasons why he thinks that the boss does in fact accept it as an issue for intervention.

> I didn't have a chance to tell the managing director with the personnel director there, that that was a real major issue — but I think he knows it. I suspect he knows it — I think that's why we're being used.

Another consultant whom we interviewed was in an organizational situation where the issues to be used as foci for intervention had to be licensed by a hierarchy. We quoted him in the last section, talking about the way issues came back to him after being licensed by the hierarchy, saying that the issues were:

> . . . recognizable to me, in a different form . . . it still fits within the strategic pattern of doing something within a particular field.

He made it clear that he paid attention to phrasing the issues which he put forward for licensing in such a way that they came back in a form which he still found acceptable. He spoke of his messages

> coinciding with someone else's intervention at a different level, going in to a great mishmash, and coming back as a proposal which, as I say, would fit into a strategy that I'm working at.

The action of parties in an organization are affected not by their power-positions as seen by some objective observer, but rather their own 'subjective' perceptions of that power. One group of consultants told us about a situation in which they had, for a long time, believed themselves to be relatively low in power, and in which they were treading with extreme caution, because if they proposed issues for intervention which were not then accepted, they would have even less power. They then realized that the people with whom they were dealing were under orders to cooperate with them, and that actually their power to define the issues and choose the interventions in the situation was very great. They considered it a tactical mistake on the part of the person who had let them know this to give them the information, but once having got the information they intended to use it, and to act according to their new perception of their power. It is interesting to compare this event with the description by Argyris (1970), of a more collaborative process, where the object is to

> . . . involve the clients in the introduction, design, execution, feedback, and evaluation of any and all aspects of the programme and to provide for them many opportunities for psychological success, feelings of essentiality, development of confidence and trust in others, and effective group relations.

There are different problems, of course, where someone wishes to define power itself as being an issue for an intervention, where they have to reckon with

> . . . how sensitized people are to protecting their own boundaries and their own power, which is very much the issue that you're working with at the centre of a multi-national, nothing to do with logic, but power. Who's got the most power?

It may be very difficult to persuade those who have the most power that they would wish power to be opened up as an issue for an intervention in their organization. Sometimes this is difficult because the people involved are not very interested in seeing the issue opened up for intervention, as in the case of one person who told us that he had a low motivation towards such a project 'because I'm not very keen on the immediate objective, and I'm not sure about a longer term one'. Sometimes, even when people are motivated around an issue, they need persuading to open it up, or to license it to be opened up, because they do not know how it could be done safely. One consultant told us how he had persuaded a group of people to open up such an issue saying:

> There are things you are in possession of, my friends, which you are not putting up as agenda items, that you are feeling pissed off about but you are not saying—right? Now then, how are we going to take that first step of putting things on the table, because

they can't be discussed without putting them on the table?

This consultant went on to explain how the issue had been handled (and safely) through his making interventions at later stages to prevent it being brushed aside or recriminations being taken. The issue was apparently only opened successfully because of trust in him on the part of the persons concerned.

Consultants and the Politics of Issue Construction

We have said that consultants often see themselves as powerful persons in the politics and negotiation of problem construction. Within that, the different statuses of external and internal consultants in political activity about issue definition exercised some of our interviewees. For example, one internal said:

> The external, outside, disinterested onlooker, if they've got personality and are accepted, will always be more influential than someone within the organization, because I'm bound to be a threat to someone else.

To the externals, however, the indispensable role of the internal is often more apparent than it is to internal consultants. One external said about his internal:

> He will talk to you for long periods of time, rambling on, but it is important to talk to him. We feed him ideas, but we let him rewrite them into language which he sees as appropriate to the organization, and into a stance which he thinks the organization will move on, and that's been successful because he's been right more times than not.

Thus the internal consultant has the critical asset, for the politics of defining the issue which will define the intervention, of knowing the organization. As one of them put it:

> You get some information and foster the idea that someone should be discussing it, and six months later someone says 'Don't you think it would be a good idea if . . .?' and you say, 'What a good idea!' It's like advice. People usually take it in arrears . . . . Strategically, you've got to know your organization. Time and place is the whole essence of this. A brilliant idea at the wrong time doesn't get listened to, but a stupid idea at the right time, and people think it's a pearl of wisdom.

Another question which seemed important to some people in the political process was credibility. One person explained that issues from a group were or were not listened to according to the credibility of that group, and that the group gained credibility when 'they seemed to be talking about things that are of substance and not trivia'.

That this argument is likely to be circular—groups gain credibility if they are talking about things of substance, and things are seen as having substance if they are talked about by groups who are credible—does not invalidate it, but simply points out one of the reinforcing effects which tends to make the organizational power to define issues and control interventions quite a long term, stable power.

The power to define issues as being illegitimate for interventions, or even for discussion, is quite highly valued by many people, for example by the consultant who told us that 'when the issue's a fairly hot one, it gets deferred, because the power not to discuss something is a pretty powerful power'. Most commonly this is done, as suggested in that quotation, by not allowing an issue to be discussed, although without anyone actually stating that that is not allowed. This is similar to the notion of non-decision making—the power to define issues as not within the scope of discussion—identified by Bachrach and Baratz (1970). This is sometimes done openly by people like the one who told us that it was important that people should know where they stand, and that therefore he would sometimes say that 'in our view, that's not an issue within the scope of the discussions that we're prepared to have with you'. He acknowledged this to be a risky strategy, but believed it to be worthwhile for reasons partly of ethics and partly of long term trust. A more direct way of defining certain issues as not being foci for interventions which is open to external consultants and relatively independent internals, but not to most employees, is to decide that they simply will not handle issues of certain types. One consultant said:

> Well, any boss who is trying to work a flanker on his people, 'good afternoon'. I don't wish to know that.

He elaborated this by explaining that this was quite a common situation in his company, and that the position of bosses who were trying to work the flankers was quite understandable, but that he simply chose not to work with that situation. Most people most of the time, however, do not feel free to make such unilateral declarations about the political and negotiative aspects of finding issues for interventions.

Consultants and Issues

If issues are used to define interventions, then consultants who make interventions in organizations need issues if there are to be any such interventions for them to carry out. Not surprisingly, however, the idea that issues are needed if consultants are to stay in business is seldom expressed within the consulting community. There seem to be constraining social norms about this, of the same sort as those which prevent medical doctors from speaking in glowing terms of sickness and ill health. When consultants do speak of a need for issues, it is usually in some rather limited sense, as for example the need for small issues which can get them started in an organization. Thus one consultant said:

> I wish I knew how to run bad events, which might sound double-Dutch. Like I always worry about euphoria at a good event; if we have a bad event then I know we really have got trouble and there really is something to get my teeth into.

A similarly limited statement about needing issues came in the comment of an external consultant who said of one of his internals:

> I'm trying to grow him to be a professional client, because at the moment, he's an amateur client. The only way you're really going to make progress is to develop his level of awareness so that he becomes a professional client.

Here the consultant acknowledged his need for a trained, aware, professional person to bring issues to him, even if he does not acknowledge his need for issues. For some consultants it seems that what they need is the kind of definable, describable issues which give rise to projects, which in turn legitimize the presence of the consultant in the organization, like the consultant who said:

> The projects I get called in on are a way of my being used so that I have a legitimate role in the organization. But the organization development work is going on as well as working in these projects.

Sometimes this need for issues leads to a gentle persuasion being exercised on clients, as for example, with a consultant who said that his colleague was at present working with a somewhat recalcitrant group 'seeing if he could get them to think more systematically about the whole problem which exists'. The clients concerned had seemingly failed to recognize the 'problem that existed' (as defined by the consultants), but the consultants were continuing, in the confidence that they knew best, to persuade those clients that the problem did exist. Some consultants are more explicit about the selling aspect of their activities, like the one who said:

> In a field like OD we're trying to introduce new concepts, then we tend to become a little bit like salesmen, and not only salesmen but salesmen in a foreign language.

It seems unlikely that many consultants would deny that they need issues, in the sense in which we are using the word. What is perhaps more surprising is how frequently they find themselves, for reasons which they often do not seem to want to explore, needing definable issues or problems to work with. It may be that such smaller, more identifiable issues are valued mainly for the feelings of security which they can bring. We were told about one possible reason for this in a previous research project (Sims, 1978), by a person who said:

> Small projects like mine found quite a bit of favour at the start with the group, simply because it was easier to deal with small individual items like that than to decide at the beginning how to tackle the larger. (p.11, 26)

Quite often a consultant is able to work in a situation without being clear about what the issue is. However, on occasions the consultant may suggest that some members of the organization know more than he does and are clearer than he is, and this can lead to anxiety and suspicion on the part of the consultant that he is being used to further the ends of some party to the intervention, but without knowing what these ends are. For example, one consultant who was heading a project team in a particular intervention told us:

> I knew nothing about the place, or what the managing director wants from the project. And that is still the situation—I don't know what he's expecting from it. . . . There's no point in asking me questions, because I still don't know the answers.

Six months later, the same person, speaking of the same project, said:

> You know that I had a difficulty, I still don't really know, for instance, what the managing director expected out of it—What was he after? What did he want out of it? What was I trying to reach with him?

The consultant was clearly uncomfortable about not knowing at all what issues the managing director had in mind in approving and collaborating with the project, but the consultant had not been so uncomfortable or so debilitated by this lack of knowledge that he had not been able to carry the project through as head of the team. In fact he told us later that he had not been uncomfortable at all until we started asking him questions about it, because he had not been aware of it.

Sometimes the consultant's actions can be almost the converse of this, where he himself defines the issues for intervention and then persuades the parties within the organization to accept his definitions. This was typified by the consultant who was coopted on to the Executive Board of a client company, and said:

One of the things I persuaded them to do was to start looking at not just operational issues, but what might be things that could be on the horizon.

In this case, the consultant is doing something a little different in that he is not so much defining the issues that his client should consider for intervention, but rather trying to bring about a redefinition of the area in which his client looks for issues. Here the consultant is not persuading his client that a specific issue should be handled, and from the quotation above there is no indication that the consultant thought he knew what issues should be handled. What he did was to work with a steering group of clients to 'dream up' change objectives in the use of human resources. These were then used rather like terms of reference, which are very often boundaries for the area in which a person or a group is authorized to look for issues. This emerged as quite a significant pattern amongst the consultants we talked to, that they used their influence to affect the areas in which issues were defined, rather than the definition of specific issues. Another example of this was described to us as follows:

The way we worked was, we sat down and we, as a Steering Group, said 'if we look at the way human resources are used in the lab, and the things that OD could offer, what would we most like to see happen? What would be the most desirable change objectives?' We dreamed those up ourselves, we tested them around with the lab director and other people, and we got agreement.

At the same time, it is not uncommon to hear consultants describe situations in which they were responsible for the definition of specific issues — 'We virtually prescribed for them what we wanted to do.' Some consultants seemed to have fairly clear rules for themselves about when such definition was and was not legitimate. Thus a person who chooses to make most of his projects serve both as research and consultancy said that:

the only difficulty with combining research and consultancy is that in consultancy I have to start from their problems and their definition of the situation. I cannot test techniques until they can be seen to be useful.

So for this person it was legitimate to define the issues for the persons and the organization he was working with, so long as they were not paying him. Another frequent pattern is for the consultant to feel it legitimate to persuade clients to redefine problems:

I said I didn't think they understood the problems of their depart- ment. When we discussed this for a while they seemed to come round to that view, they thought they had a perception of what the problems were, but really if you looked right down in the department that they probably didn't know what people felt.

Surrogate Issues

Issues, we have said, are most helpfully looked at as being constructions through which the persons whose issues they are understand their situations. The issues that a person sees in a situation may appear to be 'right' or 'wrong', 'real' or 'unreal' to an observer, but that observer can never be as much of an expert on the person's situation as the person is himself. There is thus something rather strange about one person saying that another is not seeing the 'right' or 'real' issue. Similarly, a person's understanding of his world is constantly changing, both because of new events and because of new ways of understanding. Despite all this, there seems to be a separable category of 'surrogate' issues, where one may believe that someone (or oneself) has replaced one issue with another not because they have reconstructed the issue from their situation, or because they have a different way of seeing it, but through a deliberate or careless desire not to cope at present with the implications of the issue that has been displaced. Most of us can recognize this distinction from occasions when we have been questioned on an issue that we have been working on, and have become uncomfortable because we 'know deep down' that our energies have been going somewhere other than where we intended. Similarly, sometimes any or all of the parties involved in an intervention seem to become sidetracked from the issue which was originally used to define that intervention, and become preoccupied instead with some other issue. For a consultant, this can often be the issue of credibility. For example:

> I think the main objective was achieved, and that was the acceptance of the credibility of the report itself.

That intervention project had, of course, started off by being defined in terms of a more substantive, less instrumental, issue than simply maintaining and enhancing the credibility of the consultants.

Sometimes one or more parties adopt an 'If I were going there, I wouldn't start from here' approach, and a preliminary issue is set up, for example, a change in the attitude or behaviour of some party, so that the intervention can then proceed. If the intermediate issue proved intractable the original issue may never be reached. In one case a consultant told us about a person in a client organization:

> We've been drilling him in his way of working, and giving him some expert help, hoping to then move from there into a client-centred approach; but of course he wasn't prepared to listen.

Anyway, I said we weren't going to work there any more, and that
was it.

The most frequent ways we met of displacing issues with surrogates were
where an intermediate organizational objective was set up, of the sort which
could never be said to be fully attained, but which could be approached
without limit. We found two principal ways in which this was done.

The first of these two favourite approaches is to set up a steering group,
which is meant to guide the progress of the intervention, and then to redefine
the issue as being to improve the performance, behaviour, processes, etc. of
the steering group. The implicit assumption here seems to be that a steering
group whose workings are less than perfect cannot profitably guide an
intervention into the workings of other parts of the organization. As members
of the steering group become more aware of the factors which interest their
OD consultants, so they begin to see and feel a lot of issues in the working of
their group which would not have occurred to them before. These issues are
often sufficiently new, exciting, and salient to them to predominate over
whatever remote organizational issue the steering group was originally
convened to consider. Also, interventions within the steering group are likely
to be less threatening both for the group and for the consultants.

The second major diversionary tactic for the replacing of issues with
surrogate issues is the belief that the consultant could handle the issues, but for
some good and often infinitely extendable reason, not yet. Thus some
consultants seemed to spend much of their time trying to gain the ear of higher
and higher members of the organization, seeing such projects as they were
involved in for the mean time as not being of major significance because they
are not yet working with highly-placed persons. In such cases it can happen
that by the time the consultant has collected the ears of the whole hierarchy,
some significant members of that hierarchy move to other jobs, and he has to
find a way of talking to their replacements. It would seem that such a process,
if carefully managed by the consultant, need never end.

What we have said about surrogate issues may sound like a denigration of
those consultants whom we saw as going through this process of issue
displacement. We believe that this activity often deserves criticism, and that it
may be a major contributor to the ineffectiveness of some consultants and
some interventions. Having cast that first stone, however, we should recognize
that probably all of us, on occasions, engage in the displacing of large, hard,
difficult, or intractible issues with relatively simple, programmable issues. It is
common, we suspect, for persons who are defining issues for themselves from
their situations, for a person who is too busy, or who has a personal problem
current, or who has already identified a large and hairy issue the day before, to
define a much smaller, simpler issue than he would otherwise have done. To
do so cannot of course be described as a mistake, because there are no good
grounds to attribute 'correctness' to one definition rather than another.
However, these different definitions, redefinitions, degenerations, or

introductions of surrogate issues will significantly affect the course which an intervention takes, and the satisfaction which is given by it.

So, Where do Interventions Come From?

In this chapter, we have presented a small part of the mass of data which we collected and analysed in our research, and on which our thinking and theorizing was based. We found that many statements in the comments given by interviewees tallied with other research (see for example Allison, 1971; Hewitt and Hall, 1973; Kepner and Tregor, 1965; and Pounds, 1969), in showing that different persons define quite different issues in a situation, and that where issues have to be agreed amongst a group of persons, as is almost always the case in an organizational intervention, then there is a complicated process of trading, negotiation and other forms of internal politicking around the reaching of an agreement in a group or team as to what the problem shall be held to be (Jones, Eden, and Sims, 1979). The issue which is chosen for an intervention has considerable significance for the subsequent conduct of that intervention, a point which we make both on the basis that it is grounded in the theories of the consultants and managers whom we interviewed and that it is well documented in previous literature, for example by Ackoff (1974) who says:

> We fail more often because we solve the wrong problem than because we get the wrong solution to the right problem (p.8)

The potentially devastating effects of changing the question to which an answer is being sought are illustrated by Tuffield (1977), who considers the often discussed issue of how Britain can regain its place as a major industrial nation. Tuffield effectively demolishes this issue by the use of evidence which suggests that Britain never was a major industrial nation; when the issue changes as radically as this, the whole debate around the issue must change equally. We choose the example of Tuffield's work because it is on a topic which many people discuss, and on which many of our readers will have views. However, the same radical change in debate produced by a change in issue is a familiar experience in many organizational settings, and this is why it is important to consider where an issue for intervention comes from and how it is developed to the point where it is recognized and agreed as being such an issue.

We have sought to show that consultants are believed, by themselves and others, to have enormous power in this matter of issue definition. One group like to protect and seek to enhance this power, a second group seek to make use of that power but only to encourage reconstruction, not to influence the direction, a third group seem to wish to abdicate that power, whilst a fourth group attempt to use their power to enforce participative procedures. In all cases the power relationship seems to be taken as a fact of life. This will be seen as a bad thing by those who believe that the consultant should discover what the client's problem is, and work on that. However, this research and previous work that we have done leads us to question whether that is ever possible, even assuming that it would be desirable. Eden and Sims (1979) suggested that the nearest to working on a client issue that a consultant could ever hope to achieve was to negotiate with the client an issue which was not strictly either the client's issue or the consultant's issue, but which was of interest to both, and which, if worked on, was seen as likely to produce outcomes that were of interest to both. It may be that the notions of starting from where the client is, and of working with the client's issues were set forth by the first generation of Organization Development practitioners as ideals, and have been taken up by subsequent generations as essentials of the orthodox creed. This certainly does seem to be a major example of the conceptual disjunction between the spoken words with which people describe what should be, and the other spoken words with which people describe what they do. (We say more about the concept of conceptual disjunction in Chapter 7).

From what we have said, it may be necessary to question whether the notions of finding the issues for intervention that have been current in the OD field have been too simplistic. Is it really so important to work with a problem which the client feels he has, or, given that this seems to be just about impossible, is it better to work with an issue which the consultant believes he is good at working with, regardless of the client's felt needs (or lack of them)? Are the goals of reflective, non-directive data gathering for diagnosis attainable at all without the consultant departing altogether? If they are not attainable, is it not time that we acknowledged this and owned up to the degree of personal control which we experience when engaged in Organization Development? On the other hand, can consultants build up their skills of reconstructing what the client's felt issues might be from the much adapted versions of these issues which they hear in organizational meetings? And even if consultants do need issues to the extent that they sometimes manufacture them (although their formal role is to dispose of them rather than to make them) which of us could honestly say that we do not do that repeatedly in our personal and organizational lives? If it is the case that ultimately we 'make' the issues that we work on, that they are our own constructions for ourselves, and ultimately within our control, does this not suggest that the range of choices open to us in the way we handle those issues is much greater than the range within which we usually operate? If this is the case, this suggests the possibility of whole new areas of intervention for consultants, where they attempt to intervene not simply to dispose of issues defined by their clients, but to facilitate and affect the processes of issue definition (Sims and Jones, 1981). Success in such projects might consist in the evolution and development, rather than the solution and disposal, of a problem. This would imply, consistently with the intuitions of many consumers of interventions, that a successful intervention may have more to do with changes in the awareness of the parties to it than with 'action' outcomes.

References

Ackoff, R. (1974). *Redesigning the Future*, New York: Wiley.

Allison, G. T. (1971). *Essence of Decision*, Waltham: Little Brown.

Argyris, C. (1970). *Intervention Theory and Method*, Reading, Massachusetts: Addison-Wesley.

Bachrach, P., and Baratz, M. S. (1970). *Power and Poverty: Theory and Practice*, New York: Oxford University Press.

Eden, C., and Sims, D. (1979). On the nature of problems in consulting practice. *Omega*, **7**, No. 2, 119–127.

Hewitt, J. P., and Hall, P. M. (1973). Social problems, problematic situations, and quasi-theories. *American Sociological Review*, **38**, 367–374.

Jones, S., Eden, C., and Sims, D. (1979). Subjectivity and organizational politics in policy analysis. *Policy and Politics*, **7**, No. 2, 145–163.

Kepner, C. H., and Tregoe, B. B. (1965). *The Rational Manager*, New York: McGraw-Hill.

Mangham, I. (1977). Definitions, interactions, and disengagement. *Small Group Behaviour*, **8**, No. 4, 487–510.

Merton, R. K. (1947). The machine, the worker, and the engineer. *Science*, **105**, No. 2717, 79–84.

Pounds, W. F. (1969). The process of problem finding. *Industrial Management Review*, **11**, No. 1, 1–19.

Sims, D. (1978). Problem construction in teams. *Ph.D. Thesis*, University of Bath.

Sims, D. (1979). A framework for understanding the definition and formulation of problems in teams. *Human Relations*, **32**, No. 11, 909–921.

Sims, D., and Jones, S. (1981). Explicit problem modelling—an intervention strategy. *Group and Organization Studies*, forthcoming.

Tuffield, D. (1977). *Britain is an Industrial Nation—the Content of a Myth*, University of Bath: Centre for the Study of Organizational Change and Development.

Chapter 6

Planned Change: A Notion of Convenience

Introduction

In this chapter we shall attempt to distinguish what we consider to be the myth of planned change in OD from the reality of practice portrayed by those we interviewed.

In the early literature, and still when many OD practitioners talk about their art, 'planned change', and 'organization development' are used almost interchangeably, where planned change is understood to involve a systematic approach to change and the use of rational, sequential models as blueprints for interventions. However, we found it to be both a notion of limited practical utility and an inappropriate description of the activities of many consultants.

We believe, therefore, that there is a gap between the literature of OD and the practices of interventionists, which may mislead anyone trying to become a practitioner or seeking some insight into the methods used by consultants.

On the basis of our research we argue for an alternative notion, namely that OD as practised consists largely of activities aimed at making change 'plannable'. By this we mean that these activities contribute to creating awareness among organization members of the possibilities for them to engage in change, and to making change a manageable phenomenon.

We begin the chapter with a review of the use and meaning of 'planned change' in the literature. After noting criticisms of some written versions of OD, we consider our data, looking at the involvement of the interviewees with planned change and at the alternative conceptions of change they described. Then we discuss what our findings may indicate about the development of OD before summarizing and concluding our argument.

Planned Change in the Literature

OD seems to have started life in an era when the prevailing concerns of organizations lay in the perceived increasing rate and prominence of change. Bennis (1966), for example, said:

> OD is a response to change, a complex educational strategy intended to change the beliefs, attitudes, values, and structure of organizations so that they can better adapt to new technologies,

markets, and challenges and the dizzying rate of change itself.

The theme of OD as a way of adjusting to the 'new phenomenon of change was echoed by Burke (1972):

> It . . . involves a transition from a culture which resists change to one that promotes the planning and employment of procedures which assist the organization in adapting to needed changes on a day-to-day basis.

We might have to return to that era in order to understand quite why the need for these change efforts to be planned and systematic was emphasized. It seems that the commitment to planning was part of a desire to be in control of events, rather than be directed by them. Whatever the rationale, the value is evident in statements about the way OD was to be conducted. Bennis (1966) wrote:

> First of all, it (OD) is an educational strategy to bring about a planned organizational change.

And Burke (1972) said:

> Organizational Development is a process of planned change.

Burke (1972) also sounded a note of caution, suggesting that an interest in effectiveness was not the only justification for a planned approach:

> A risk which exists is that OD specialists may take any and all techniques for change and have no systematic change effort.

which implies that an absence of planning would make OD less credible at a time when it was trying to establish itself as a legitimate specialism.

The principle of the need for planned change was reflected in the theoretical models of OD that began to emerge. OD was portrayed as having a number of distinct phases—orderly, prescribed stages that would apply to any change event. Beckhard (1969) for instance, outlined a five-stage model of change, consisting of diagnosis, strategy, planning, education consulting and training, and evaluation. Further examples were produced by Rogers (1972), Blake and Mouton (1969), and others.

These models apparently acted both as an official guide to the interventionist and as a description of the way change came about. A feature of most of them was their division into two general, higher-order phases; first, a broad-based educative scheme, which was considered a necessary preliminary to the second, consisting of more problem-specific activities.

We have seen in the literature, then, an espousal of planned, systematic approaches to OD. What we understand by 'planned change', and what we shall be referring to throughout the chapter, is a style of OD that is based on a prescribed model. The model dictates the stages that are to be gone through in order to achieve the stated objective of change, as well as the sequence in which they are to be tackled. The model is assumed to be applicable to any situation the consultant might be called on to intervene in.

Despite the preoccupation with planned change in OD, its ideas and models have not gone without criticism. Three questions in particular represent the doubts that have been expressed:

1. Are the models useful as guides to practitioners?
2. Are the terms and concepts appropriate to the phenomena OD claims to deal with?
3. Do the models describe what practitioners do?

As we have seen, Bennis was an advocate of 'planned change', and his emphasis on OD as an educational strategy implied that interventionists would have the time and resources to control the change effort. However, by the mid-1970s Bennis (1975) had realized a discrepancy between this view and what he saw happening in organizations. He suggested that adherence to the theoretical models of OD would cause the consultant to miss important aspects of organizational life.

> . . . it is not looking at the right things. It is not looking at the politics of what is happening at the boundaries of organizations.

It seems that continual mobilization of the literature's descriptions may lure interventionists into activities that are removed from the pragmatic requirements of change situations.

Bennis (1975) also raises the second question about OD:

> It lacks a certain conceptual bite which would illuminate in more detail what is happening in organizations right now.

Kahn (1974), for example, has criticized the adoption from other disciplines of terms such as 'independent variables'. This may be encouraging practitioners to fit OD problems into a pre-existing conceptual structure, thus obstructing the development of a terminology grounded in the area itself.

It is also pertinent to ask whether practitioners do act on the basis of these models. Planned change seems to be a particularly strong 'espoused theory', but is it a 'theory in use?' Weisbord (1974) wrote:

> My conclusion is that there is a vast gap between OD as researched and written down, and OD as actually practised.

And McLean (1978) considered that models of social change in OD are little more than

pious representations bordering on the fictitious.

So, if the descriptions in the literature are inaccurate, what activities do consultants actually engage in? And if planned change models are not adhered to, how useful are they to interventionists? We turn now to our research findings.

Practitioners' Activities

From our research we identified two contrasting clusters of consulting activities, which we called 'closed loop' and 'ad hoc'. Closed loop activities seemed to adhere to the notions and nostrums in the literature, and so may be described as planned change, although they did not go through all the stages of the models. Ad hoc activities, on the other hand, appeared to be unrelated to any prescribed strategy or sequential model. They represented a more contingent, opportunistic approach to interventions.

Closed Loop Activities

The activities in this grouping were associated with terms such as 'strategy', 'stages', 'objectives', and 'plans'. This in itself might not be significant, for we found that the usage of words such as these varied; however, the activities were constituents of an overall pattern which appeared to be independent of a particular situation, and which was conceived of as a stage-by-stage operation.

The continued existence of these activities shows that 'planned change' has not ceased altogether to describe current practice; yet it lends support to the view that models based on this notion are inappropriate for the interventionist, for we found that closed loop activities became diverted from their aim of effecting change. The term 'closed loop' refers to the way a change programme would proceed through a number of stages of the particular model being followed, but loop back to the beginning of a sequence before reaching the end.

This diversion could occur in different ways. First, the change effort could be typified by the tenet of 'insufficient data for action'. In these cases the steps of client contact, data collection, and analysis and feedback of the results were rounded off by the conclusion that there was a need to collect more data.

A second form of diversion seems in part to be a consequence of the emphasis of theoretical models on education before action. An education programme such as a career-planning exercise, ostensibly set up as a preliminary to change, may seduce the attentions and energy of the interventionist so that it becomes the end rather than the means.

Third, it is common for a steering group of organization members to be established to be versed in the skills of change management. The idea here is for the members of the organization to be left in charge of, and with the ability to proceed with, their own change programme. What seems to happen, however, is that the problems the members of the steering group have with their own processes begin to overshadow the problem they originally set out to work on, which is then neglected.

An example of the last form of delay is provided by a case study of events which took place in one plant over the course of a year or so.

1. External consultants were brought in by the internal to help with development; they carried out a survey in the plant and identified problems people had in various parts of the organization. These they hoped to solve.
2. Subsequently a steering group was set up (though not including the people with the problems) to help to solve the problems but, having no precise terms of reference, they found themselves uncertain how to proceed.
3. They brought back the external consultants who worked with them to enable them to function more effectively as a group. They began to discuss how to disseminate the group skills they were developing to other people in the plant.
4. At this stage, however, they realized that they were not confident about what they, as a temporary and unofficial part of the organization structure, actually had the power to do and were therefore uncertain whether they could resolve the substantive problems they were supposed to deal with.
5. Meanwhile the problems originally diagnosed in the plant remained unsolved.

Thus, while we have observed that planned change models are still followed, it seems that they are insufficient as guides for practitioners. We think that two things may contribute to this outcome. First, the sort of change model that is to be found in the literature typically starts with a number of stages such as: developing awareness of a need to change; contracting with clients to work on the felt need; diagnosis; and data collection and feedback — activities for which there are well-established methodologies and books available explaining how to proceed. But when we reach the 'action plan' stage the literature gives little guidance except in general terms. Any recommendations that are made tend to be at the level of objectives, desired states to be attained, with very little suggestion of how they are to be reached.

The second factor is the assumption that a change programme necessarily contains an action plan. Interventionists concern themselves with providing a visible, concrete outcome for their efforts, seeing this as proof to the organization of their competence and effectiveness. When 'hard' changes cannot be achieved — perhaps due in part to their absence of guidance in the literature — consultants switch their attention to the perfection of the education programme or of the performance of a steering group; action's sake.

Ad hoc Activities

Ad hoc activities contrasted with closed loop activities by being unrelated to any theoretical, programmatic model. Instead we would characterize them as elements of a repertoire, used as and when the interventionist found them appropriate. In practice these consultants' activities seemed to be opportunistic and their working methods pragmatic. A change effort was accelerated or slowed down according to their reading of the situation, and such changes as did occur took place apparently expediently as the right circumstances presented themselves.

The interviewees spoke in terms of concepts like 'strategies', 'plans', and 'objectives', but they appeared to be using them in a general, non-specific way. They were more a means of simplifying and making comprehensible the complexity with which they were dealing and the long time spans they appeared to work to. One person expressed his goal as:

> To improve the processes of participation in this company

but he did not have a sequence of activities to be followed step by step in pursuit of this. Another consultant, talking about a change proposal put forward within the organization, illustrates that strategies and objectives were hardly blueprints for action in every case:

> It's recognizable to me, you know, it still fits within the strategic pattern of doing something in a particular field, but comes back in an entirely different form . . . but I know it still meets some of the objectives that I have sought to get.

Here the strategic pattern is a kind of reference, a description of the types of events and changes that will contribute to the objectives. It doesn't define what must be done but helps the consultant see each activity in the context of the broad goal.

Interventionists often did have plans, and notions of stages they were going through; but, as in the following quote, these referred only to the next few moves, not to a section of a prescribed programme:

> We were closely involved throughout the early stages of planning, and getting the decision-making process underway. The next two or three steps, none of us were really thinking that far ahead, there are enough problems to deal with there without going in for some theoretical strategy.

We can see, then, that plans and objectives did have a part to play, but not in the way the literature would lead us to expect. The last quote suggests that the constraints and complexities of the situation were too great for the implementation of a simplified, planned programme.

This reflects another feature of ad hoc activities; practitioners demonstrated a concern with understanding the context of an intervention — the idiosyncrasies and practicalities of the situation. One consultant indicated the need for assessing the characteristics of each organization, even where one organization appeared to be very similar to another.

> I worked in another pharmaceutical company doing an identical job before I came here — literally identical — there's not many pharmaceutical companies which are absolutely identical; identical in organization at the top, identical in the product range, very similar in their general approach to organization — but they are two different organizations, totally different organizations . . . and that's why I say there is a uniqueness in any organization and you've *got* to develop the ways and means and process around that uniqueness.

The principle of undertaking diagnostic investigation — identifying the centres of power, seeking information, and assessing the political climate and the areas of support and resistance — was reflected in accounts of the ways plans were drawn up. For example:

> So I'm going to see him next week when we will discuss all of it in more detail and try and come up with some sort of plan of where we want to go, which will inevitably mean involving his boss and also his colleague, who I don't think will be very receptive at all, so it's working out a strategy.

This certainly contradicts the Bennis criticism, quoted earlier in this chapter, that OD fails to allow for the political nature of organizations. In addition, the idea of working out a strategy contrasts tellingly with the version in the literature, and indicates an inherent difficulty with the notion of planned change; it is essentially a theoretical, abstract approach — when used, its stages and phases seem to be imposed upon the situation, and the organization and its issues are seen in terms of the theory. One person summed up these limitations:

> . . . so that it doesn't seem planned, etc., because I don't personally believe you can do that. You can have some sort of overall framework but in terms of how you get there, or the speed you get there, or whatever, it has to depend on how the process is going and the role that everyone is planning in that.

Thus interventionists may work to general goals and construct plans for each particular situation because the models in the literature are inappropriate, unable to cope with the complexities and contingencies found in the act of consulting.

There is another sense in which the interventionist using planned change is led to impose on the situation; not because the plan is abstract, but because it requires someone to direct and control its application.

> At one time OD used to be you know the OD consultant doing his thing; data gathering, or whatever else, then team-working or being centre stage which is not right, which is really him imposing himself on the situation. He imposes his values onto an organization situation, and he's not encouraging the organization to make its own choice.

We found that, with ad hoc consulting, interviewees preferred a less central role. The indirect approach they described has parallels with the role of cultivator, which we discussed in Chapter 3. For example:

> You start and it grows till you end up with something and you take it up one more level and it sort of grows into the organization rather than imposing something from the top, it is very much a self-generating activity.

Another consultant said:

> I sought to persuade them to do something about it, and they said they would, and then for six months they didn't and then suddenly out of the blue they had a meeting and said 'well we really ought to get on with it'.

Connected with this idea is the way the ad hoc style involved the consultant in urging people to take a wider perspective on their own organizations; to be critical, to look ahead, and to anticipate issues — something we might expect a consultant working from planned change to retain expertise in. One interviewee said:

> I call it organization effectiveness to distinguish it from OD as such. It tries to remain task-centred. It is not the OD you find in the literature. It becomes OD work in the way in which we use it, which is really a way of examining business assumptions of all kinds.

Here we can see the consultant's efforts being applied to creating conditions in which the members of the organization become more aware of the circumstances in which they find themselves — both inside the organization and in the environment. Another consultant remarked:

> One of the things I persuaded them to do was to start looking at, not just operational issues, but what might be things that

could be on the horizon. Dimly on the horizon at that time were ideas about participation.

This quote also provides a clue to an important feature of ad hoc consulting. While the natural changes and events in an organization might be considered obstructions to the implementation of planned change models — forcing delays and unwanted changes of strategy — our interviewees treated these as opportunities. Indeed, they were less an adjunct to ad hoc consulting than a central part of it.

We pick up things that will rub together. To start from the idea of problem definition would be too long winded, we must rather look for opportunities. These are big interdependent systems, what one does — most of it — is opportunistic.

This signifies a willingness to abandon the idea of being in control of a programme and instead take advantage of whatever comes along. One consequence of this is that the focus of the consulting activities can change over time. As one interviewee put it:

So real change really means stepping into the unknown and therefore the documentation of an OD development becomes incredibly difficult for that reason. What you are trying to describe in month nine bears little relation to what you thought you were doing in month one.

Ad hoc consulting therefore involves much more flexibility in response than planned change. We found that people believed that situations can change dramatically and haphazardly, and an opportunistic approach was typified by a reluctance to be committed to rigid objectives or plans. For example:

I always have several action plan strategies which I use because the situation changes over time.

Another consultant said:

I've learned the hard way that new objectives emerge, therefore it is definitely dangerous to start with all your objectives laid out.

Thus the emphasis of consultants' work shifted as the environment altered, and changes took place as circumstances created opportunities.

In this section we have described two kinds of consulting activity. The first, which we termed 'closed loop' showed an adherence to the principles of planned change without managing to achieve its objectives. The second, called 'ad hoc', might have retained an aura of planning but its practices were quite different from those described in the literature. In the next section we discuss our findings and offer what we believe to be a more suitable description of OD as it is practised.

The Implications of Current Practice

Although the literature of OD leads one to believe that 'planned change' describes the way consultants work, our findings suggest that the notion is of limited utility. The interviewees portrayed planned change models as too abstract and inflexible for the complex task of organization development, and pointed out that their use leads to the imposition of inappropriate values and interpretations in situations.

It seems to us that planned change models may be an historical way of making sense of interventions; the results of applying a retrospective logic to events and actions. Our interviewees, for example, could and sometimes did place a sequential logic on their activities when giving accounts of their projects. However, this has not been made clear by the literature, and people may have assumed that these orderly models describe how interventions *should* be conducted. So, while the literature may give some insight to those who knew nothing of OD, it can lead the inexperienced into closed loop activities.

Meanwhile, the language and values of planned change are being perpetuated. Although consultants participating in ad hoc activities used terms like 'strategy' and 'objective' in a distinctive way, the fact that these continue to be the currency of conversation between interventionists sustains the impression that the models themselves are stll being employed.

'Planning' is, itself, a value-laden word. During a feedback session some people objected to our use of the term 'ad hoc' for some of their activities because they felt it implied that they had no particular skills, that they didn't know what they were doing. Our intention was rather to typify the pragmatic, contingent nature of these activities, but that people did object indicates some commitment to the value of planning. Any approach for which the label 'planned' is rejected is assumed to be quite *un*planned—which, in turn, has connotations of unprofessionalism, unpreparedness, and even incompetence. This is a considerable obstacle for any attempt to replace accepted notions with more appropriate alternatives.

Despite the persistence of notions of planned change, our findings suggest that OD has taken a direction different from that indicated by the literature. We offer an alternative notion; current OD practice might instead be described as largely a collection of activities designed to make change 'plannable'. This refers to the way consultants are helping their clients to come to terms with the complexity of change, enabling them to recognize opportunities and constraints, and encouraging an attitude that treats change as a challenge that can be tackled with success. In this way change becomes a manageable phenomenon.

In support of this alternative notion, we found that many of the activities undertaken by consultants were aimed at creating awareness among organization members more than at actually bringing change about. This was essentially the emphasis of both ad hoc and closed loop activities. In the case of the ad hoc, we recall from the previous section that consultants encouraged clients to take responsibility for the development of ideas; that the consultants' pragmatic attitude would help the client to recognize and capitalize on opportunities; and that consultants tried to persuade clients to look ahead, to identify and think about issues that might need attention in the future.

While closed loop activities were ostensibly elements of a plan intended actively to bring change about, in practice the stages completed were educative rather than action-based. However, there seems to have been a movement away from the broad, abstracted educational programmes of planned change. These involved a particular kind of awareness — awareness of theoretical concepts, definitions and perspectives — that was learned in isolation from the issues in question. The creation of this form of awareness was considered to be a prerequisite for the problem-solving process.

This theoretical kind of training is seen as less appropriate now. Both consultants — recognizing the shortcomings of an approach that involves selling the definitions and models of the literature — and clients — requiring training more directly relevant to their problems — are coming to prefer task-centred activities. These involve learning-by-doing, acquiring skills through dealing with live issues, and the awareness, which is of possibilities, constraints and opportunities, is created for a purpose, not as an end in itself. This is the emphasis of ad hoc activities, where the behavioural sciences are the underpinning rather than the focus.

This leaves us with one area to which OD may need to pay more attention. If, as we have suggested, OD currently focuses on making change plannable, where does that leave the action stage? Is this something that is being neglected but which should be an important part of OD? Or is an emphasis on action a hangover from the models of planned change? Some consultants may believe that increased awareness will, of itself, permeate the organization in the form of individual changes. Yet it may be that awareness is not a sufficient condition for change; we feel there is a need to give more consideration to the question of how increased awareness may lead to change rather than resting on the assumption that it does. We are not suggesting that creating awareness is not a legitimate activity for interventionists, but that expectations about what it is likely to achieve could be examined in the light of its apparent outcomes.

Other consultants may consider their role to stop short of action, leaving the client capable of and responsible for implementing change. Again, without coming down either for or against such an approach, we should like to draw attention to assumptions about the action stage. As we noted above, the inclusion of action phases in models of intervention in the literature may lead people to believe that this is an essential element of consultancy. We think more consideration needs to be given to the question of whether an action stage is always necessary; at least so that consultants can avoid engaging in action for action's sake. Continuing to demonstrate efficacy in this way both manifests and sustains a myth about what the consultant's role should be.

On the other hand, recognizing that action need not be undertaken does not amount to placing it outside the scope of OD. Clients may still need help at this stage, and we have come across instances when interventionists could and did give this; yet the consultants concerned, who seemed to be working from hunch and intuition, found it hard to describe what they did or how this might lead to change. We have commented earlier that the literature fails to give explicit guidance about the transition from education to action, and once more we suggest that more attention be given to this area. In particular we would note that the consultant's role in the action stage need not be directive; facilitating change, by arranging for the availability of resources and gaining the support of key persons, may be an appropriate activity.

Conclusion

Our intention in this chapter was to examine the notion of planned change. Our findings lead us to the conclusion that this is an inadequate description of OD as it is practised; it might be more accurate to say that most OD activities are aimed at making change plannable and manageable. OD has been evolved by some people into a set of notions and activities quite different from those to be found in the literature, yet still intelligible and possessing their own consistency.

This misdescription makes planned change models inappropriate as guides for the interventionist, and we have seen that adherence to them may lead to closed loop activities. The ad hoc consulting activities represented a move away from the orthodoxy of planned change, ceasing to rely on prescribed models and working instead from the characteristics of and opportunities in each situation.

Analysis of the application of terms such as 'planning' and 'strategy' demonstrates that there is a need for frequent re-examination of the meaning of the body of OD knowledge in the light of current developments since it can be interpreted erroneously by people who come fresh to the concepts.

We have questioned assumptions about the role of change agents and have suggested that there are choices about the extent of their involvement. Our concern here is that consultants be self-conscious of their role definitions, for this way they may avoid a number of potential traps. People whose activities are aimed at creating awareness, and who acknowledge this rather than adopting the definitions and goals of the literature, are less likely to be hampered by the idea that planned change and action are essential elements of their work.

We have noted a wish to improve our understanding of the action stage of interventions. We consider that more attention should be given to what activities such as creating awareness, which some people believe will bring change about, do achieve, and to the practices of consultants who do manage to make the transition from education to action.

We said in the introduction to this chapter that the terms 'OD' and 'planned change' are often used almost interchangeably. If we are to continue to use organization development as a description of the practices of change agents we must now see 'planned change' as something quite separate.

References

Beckhard, R. (1969). *Strategies of Organization Development*, Reading, Massachusetts: Addison-Wesley.

Bennis, W. (1966). *Changing Organizations*, New York: McGraw-Hill.

Bennis, W. (1975). Practice versus theory. *International Management*, October 1975, 41–42.

Blake, R. R., and Mouton, J. S. (1969). *Corporate Excellence Through Grid Development*, Houston, Texas: Gulf Publishing Co.

Burke, W. (1972). *The Social Technology of Organizational Development*, Fairfax, Virginia: NTL Learning Resources.

Kahn, R. L. (1974). Organization development, some problems and proposals. *Journal of Applied Behavioural Science*, 7, No. 3, 485–502.

McLean, A. J. (1978). *Organization Development: A Review of Theory Practice and Research*, University of Bath: Centre for the Study of Organization Change and Development.

Rogers, E. (1972). Change agents, clients and change. In *Creating Social Change* (Eds. G. Zaltman, P. Karler, and I. Kaufman), New York: Holt, Rinehard, and Winston, Inc.

Weisbord, M. (1974). The gap Between OD practice and theory — and publication, *Journal of Applied Behavioural Science*, 10, No. 2.

Chapter 7

Centred and Unintegrated Practitioners: A Continuum of Consulting Styles

In this chapter we address an aspect of OD consulting that took the form of a leitmotiv throughout our findings. This arose from taking, as it were, a look at our data through a horizontal plane as compared to dividing it up vertically. Viewed from this perspective we discerned a quality of consulting style that can be represented by use of a continuum, the two poles of which we have termed 'centred' and 'unintegrated'.

The chapter starts with a definition of these terms and a discussion of some important caveats before developing the concepts more fully and presenting the evidence on which we base our views. Finally we explore some of the implications of this interpretation.

The 'Centred' Consultant and the 'Unintegrated' Consultant

Explaining what we mean by these two terms is not easy. As a first attempt we borrow a passage from Carlos Casteneda (1970) who enquires of his Indian mentor, Don Juan:

> 'Take the songs, for instance. What do they mean?'
> 'Only you can decide that,' he said. 'How could I know what they mean? The protector alone can teach you his songs. If I were to tell you what they mean, it would be the same as if you learned someone else's songs.'
> 'What do you mean by that, Don Juan?'
> 'You can tell who are the phonies by listening to people singing the protector's songs. Only the songs with soul are his and were taught by him. The others are copies of other men's songs. People are sometimes as deceitful as that. They sing someone else's songs without even knowing what the songs say.'

The notion of finding one's own meaning, of refraining from copying other people's 'songs', is somewhere close to the heart of what we mean by the term 'centred'. It is a quality comprising a relatively high level of self-awareness and self-acceptance, of recognizing one's own strengths and limitations and fashioning an approach which is consistent with them. A 'centred' consultant is one who in our terms has evolved his own idiosyncratic approach to his work which is internally consistent, in that he has either resolved some of the internal contradictions and inconsistencies of his ideas and his actions, or has learned not to become too disturbed by them. Another feature of centredness is that there is an overall consistency or continuity between his ideas, his skills and his personality.

The opposite pole, which we have termed 'unintegrated', refers to an ideal type, a person who will 'sing someone else's songs without even knowing what they say', who will be working from a set of concepts and theories which are second hand, either gleaned from books and journals or from personal encounters with others. This is of course a familiar process for learning; what provides the characteristic of the unintegrated practitioner is that he has not found his *own personal meaning* in these ideas and theories, nor has he found an overall logic for organizing them in such a way as to make them compatible with his experience and congruent with his personality.

Kopp (1974) puts it nicely:

> Empty ritualistic parodies may eventually be all that are left of teachings that were once spontaneous and alive. The reification of his (the Guru's) metaphors by those who take his place may lead to the hollow appearance of continuity without the original life-giving substance of inspired teaching. (p.13)

Moreover the unintegrated practitioner seems either unable or unwilling to acknowledge major discrepancies between his espoused theories of acting and his own actual behaviour during an intervention. This quality of unresolved discrepancies is the defining characteristic of unintegrated consultants.

An external consultant summarized the essence of one such discrepancy when he said, in reference to some internal consultants:

> I think they're coming out with a lot of explicit theories but behave out of a lot of implicit needs.

Before we develop each of these ideal types in more detail it is important to us to make a statement about some of the dangers inherent in presenting our ideas in this way.

This continuum has been derived from a mass of statements that people made to us, and as such is an artefact of our creation. It is a deliberate simplification of interwoven and complex issues. The simplification is in order to clarify the ideas to ourselves and also to make it easier to present to others. The risks of doing it this way are several; that we imply that our subjects fell neatly into one or other of these categories; that we should all strive towards the centred end of the continuum and feel bad if we recognize parts of our activities that seem to be closer to the unintegrated pole, and complacent when we believe ourselves to be centred. Another risk, and one that we may not have successfully avoided, is that we, the writers, appear to be describing these phenomena from a position of smug self-satisfaction and superiority, that these are traps that other lesser mortals fall into but which we, in our wisdom, avoid.

Furthermore in early drafts of this chapter it appeared that we believed that it was 'good' to be centred and 'bad' to be unintegrated. We have sought in subsequent revisions to remove such crude value connotations from the narrative. However as may be apparent we will not have succeeded entirely in this ambition. Deep down we still do believe that it is better to be centred than unintegrated both from the viewpoint of the client organization and the consultant, and therefore such a neutrality would have been contrived and inauthentic on our part.

By way of attempting to avoid some of these traps, and to protect ourselves from justifiable accusations of oversimplification we would wish to emphasize the following.

Most of the people that we talked to, and that we quote on the following pages, displayed aspects of both qualities, centred and unintegrated, and indeed we use quotes from single individuals who illustrate the two states. This was disturbing at first since it seemed to undermine the basis of our case. Acknowledging this paradox, (having first ignored it), led us to a new, and we believe, enlightening possibility; that while most practitioners can be viewed as being characteristically closer to one extreme or the other, they can and do act in ways which are uncharacteristic for them. In this way there were people whom we considered to be centred but who at times and in certain situations acted in a clearly unintegrated fashion. Similarly there were those who, while predominantly unintegrated, on occasions seemed to epitomize centredness. We regard this as fundamentally reassuring since it confirms the fallibility of our idols and provides hope for those of us who make a mess of things from time to time.

Our purpose here, then, is not to give a pat on the back to some people for being centred nor to chastize others for being unintegrated. Rather we hope that by drawing attention to these qualities change practitioners may become more aware of what we consider to be a key feature of their style, and some of its possible implications for themselves and their clients. In particular we see it as important for the self-development and growth in competence of people who often exert considerable influence over the ideas and lives of organizational members and sometimes over the commercial future of their client companies.

The rest of the chapter develops our ideas more fully and provides supporting evidence and illustrations. There are four sections, each dealing with different manifestations of the phenomenon; the types of roles that the consultant takes, his tolerance for ambiguity, his reliance on, and use of, concepts, and finally his degree of self-awareness and self-assurance.

Description of Roles

The centred practitioner The centred consultant is clear about his role and can describe it convincingly. It is usually key in the change project, often at the centre of a network, with a considerable amount of power associated with it. He is aware of how it departs from role prescriptions to be found in the literature and is apparently relaxed about such differences.

> My role was really a pulling together of the groups of people or the various people who are working with or who have knowledge in a professional sense about what was going on, but were also providing the support to the line management who were trying to do various things.

> That's what I consider my personal role to be in the organization, that I ought to be saying things that are, perhaps, not in conformity with established patterns.

> I am a strategic doctor on, I suppose, the Dick Beckhard model, like I am much more often down the prescriptions or the general consulting route than the behavioural end. I am more often than not talking with chief executives, heads of OD, and fast moving reality testing, options suggesting . . . as against reflecting and saying I'm batting it back to them and so on.

> I'm not a skilled process consultant, I'm a sort of spider or something, and we've got skilled process consultants. Supposing it's going to build up into a long programme. It may take months or something and I can't affort to be burying myself in some country, there are too many other things to do. So I either recommend them an outside consultant or we give one of our London people a treat.

> My strategy is to let things evolve, clarify things, help people focus . . . create an umbrella, which means freedom to carry out the experiment . . . broad direction but no precise strategy . . . help in the true sense as opposed to being directive.

By contrast the unintegrated consultant role comprises a pot pourri of odds and ends, bits and pieces, as if the primary objective is to keep oneself fully occupied regardless of the extent to which the work is centrally relevant to one's role. So for example one practitioner described his immediate commitments as follows:

> Like everyone else in a bureaucracy, I'm laced around by the needs and time pressures to do things that I would rather not be doing. I'm trying to write a speech for my Managing Director, I'm trying

to do something to make our own division more cohesive, that's very urgent. There's a war going on between two people very close to me. One of my professed priorities is to re-educate my new coordinator, who is a charming man but doesn't know the first thing about what I'm doing. I'm dashing down tonight to Kent to an advanced programme there about how you do attitude surveys and what are the traps and snares and advantages and so on. I'm talking in Manchester in a couple of weeks which has a kind of Public Relations flavour. I'm going around the East Anglian companies in two weeks' time to see why our activities there are so much behind those in the South West. I'm having a fight with my boss about my next year's work programme which lists all kinds of rubbish. And I'm desperately worried about the staffing of the London unit here . . .

The sense of being helplessly overwhelmed by an avalanche of trivia and major projects all tangled together is, in our view, characteristic of the unintegrated role. There would appear to be a paradox regarding the role of unintegrated practitioners. While on the one hand they are in many senses peripheral characters, tagging on to other people's projects, enduring a piecemeal existence, they also seem to have a propensity to become entangled in a hopelessly complicated and protracted web of meetings and committees, special study groups and working parties which might be metaphorically considered as organizational fly paper. The harder they try to escape, the more firmly they become stuck!

Every time I advise somebody, he says 'Oh hell, that goes against the advice we got last week from the trade relations people!' Simple as that. And we have to start arguing about this and copying them around there, saying Jesus, we'd better get together, we'd better form a standing committee, or we'll have an ad hoc group here and a committee there and we'll copy each other more and two or three of us will go and sit together with the manager concerned, it's just built up over time.

Similarly another practitioner explained:

I get called in on all sorts of projects, it's a way of making sure that I get used as well.

Unintegrated consultants are often very busy but rarely seem to occupy centre stage:

I'm now seen to have some power in (the firm) that again is unusual to other assignments where you're doing something on the wings and people don't quite know why.

This is one of the problems, the time scale, the fact that you're allocated beginnings and ends of time.

It's difficult to get continuous work if you're selling a month at a time.

I wanted fairly quickly to get into some projects, get them working in groups on projects and I was held up for a while; the MD didn't want them to get into projects, he thought that might stir things up a bit so I was left with about three months and there was nothing I could do except call on them individually and say, 'what have you done, what have you changed?' And of course the answer to these things is nothing. It was difficult because I'd go around and the secretary was away, maybe next time!

This seeming impotence is in sharp contrast to the centrality and potency of the 'centred practitioners' whom we studied. Not only do they describe themselves as occupying a role centre stage, but they apparently establish positions of power while remaining alert to its many pitfalls:

I am apparently the key figure in this. The Plant Manager really does have to go on my say, which is something he shouldn't have let me know if he wants it to go faster.

I'm still seen as being the Guru, the chief cat.

We set up a steering group of people with whom we negotiated the project . . . We selected it . . . on the basis that the guys who were likely to have the power to defend or destroy the project, and therefore were working in the chemical area, had to be in on it.

Both Tony and myself were linking to the organization director and I was linking to the external and influencing how he operated with people like the personnel director and the operations director and the chairman of the board personnel committee and that. So my role was really a pulling together of the groups of people or the various people who are working with and have knowledge in a professional sense about what was going on but we were also providing the support to the line management who were trying to do various things.

The lesson for the consultants . . . is to watch power, implicit power, because obviously these managers knew we were spending a lot of time with the top guys and were very sensitized, I think, to that. So the power thing is both a healthy thing and a disabling thing and you've got to choose.

Tolerance for Ambiguity

The centred consultant As we have described elsewhere (see Chapter 3) some interventionists see their work in terms of years, and in some cases consider it to be a lifetime's effort.

> What I'm doing fundamentally is helping them build their own cathedrals and they probably don't even recognize it.

Many regard lasting and permanent changes to be painstakingly slow in evolving and mistrust sudden radical shifts in behaviour or attitudes. Their stance paradoxically, given their pre-occupation with change, seems to be that human systems are essentially conservative and that the predominant reaction of an organization to disturbance from any source is to re-establish equilibrium. Characteristically, centred consultants seem to have recognized this and accept it as a fact of life. For some it is an implicit acceptance while others infer it in more graphic analogies:

> So what I am doing is . . . often consenting to go three steps forward, knowing I am then going to go back four but I have to work in such a way that I'm *in*, still to live another day. And it's like skirting around the bushes . . . waiting and waiting and waiting, even though you may be confronting and confronting and confronting and confronting, so there's nothing in my book about your style at that particular point in time.

> You learn to take four steps forward and three back, and then ten forward and one back and that takes four years, only you're hoping for the Crompton step in three years' time with the client. It sometimes goes faster and you don't take so many steps back.

They operate on time scales of years, patiently building and waiting for natural opportunities.

> There has been a massive amount of, if you like, opening up and influencing going on which started really ten fifteen years ago with people like Ken James who will be our next Managing Director probably . . . . It's really a very long term movement essentially aimed at opening up, supporting any moves that they can make, suggesting moves.

There is a higher tolerance for the open-endedness of much of the work. Payoffs are rarely immediate, sometimes intangible and may only be acknowledged some years later. The centred practitioner is more able both to recognize and accept such uncertainty as in the following passages:

> I think we're mutually deciding but we don't have a master plan. We haven't even sorted out what the hell we want properly from this opportunity yet.

> We've been working on it for eighteen months now. Done nothing much but learnt a lot, learnt about processes, learnt about difficulties, learnt about behaviour, learnt about different roles.

> I don't think frankly any practitioner who says that they can look back on five years of experience and claim a hell of a lot can be really telling the truth. I believe it's like some works of art, some of those magnificent cathedrals, I think it takes more than your lifetime, like your efforts live on if they're worth it, and make an impact afterwards and some other beggar sees it. It's more like an artist who's appreciated afterwards, OK you do obviously get some recognition, acceptance of credibility, legitimacy, some warm feeling, and so on . . . I've worked with Graham as an external for many years, now a colleague for many years, and it's really only the last two years that he's beginning to see the point of some of the things I did to him, or with him. So we're building cathedrals and helping them to build cathedrals and it's a bloody long job.

Public recognition and affirmation of the value of work done is a rare luxury indeed for much OD work. Centred consultants seem to have come to terms with this fact of life, some to such an extent that they become wary of publicly acknowledged 'success' as in the following example:

> They came back from that two day exercise with a good feeling but the trouble is every event you run is bloody good and I wish I knew how to run bad events, which might sound double Dutch. Like I always worry about euphoria at a good event; if we have a bad event then I know we really have got trouble and there really is something to get my teeth into.

Such attitudes require considerable self-confidence and assurance, and may be taken for arrogance.

A further aspect of the centred consultant's tolerance for ambiguity is that they recognize the essential messiness of organizations, whereby most of the time there are far more loose ends than neatly resolved problems.

> The business of tape recording puts a funny pressure on the person telling the story, but it rather makes it sound like a completely orderly story, and it's not always like that.

Problems are not always clear cut but are often complicated, fuzzy, and something of a conundrum. Centred consultants are more likely to leave them that way for a while, almost relishing the puzzle:

> There's one major thing that is on the go and it's running into difficulty. I've seen about twenty managers so far and what I was hoping was that by talking to them I would dig out some issues and be able to use them in some catalytic way to play back at the organization. It's been made difficult by the fact that things really aren't too bad in our organization and therefore I find the data I've got I'm thinking of how could we most effectively use it—it's a puzzle! A puzzle because it's not straightforward, it's not consistent, it doesn't shine out that this needs doing or that needs doing. And like all puzzles, they get to the second place in your box.

They seem to adopt a view that much of human interaction is fundamentally problematic and will continue to be so and that perhaps the most that can be achieved is that some people will continue to confront issues and doggedly work towards temporary compromises and coalitions without the distant hope of a Utopian state. In this sense they are distinguished by the modesty of their ambition. Significantly, in this context we found that some consultants from organizations with the longest history of involvement in OD didn't think in terms of discrete OD 'projects' with a beginning, a middle and an end, but likened their involvement to a stream; flowing constantly, with periods of much turbulence, disturbance, and many hazards followed by periods of apparent calm and stillness, never certain of where they will be taken but with a belief that it will prove worthwhile. Indeed for some the real excitement and opportunities are to be found in 'shooting the rapids' of organizational life. Opportunities for development are greatest when levels of awareness are heightened by external threats:

> It's going to be some externally induced thing, like in three years time we may have some really tough frontier type legislation around participation and all.

> It's so differentiated, it is so wealthy and fat and happy that I think it's going to require a jugular vein attack by the unions in the UK to disturb it enough at the top to get any top-down energy.

To recapitulate: for us a key quality of a centred consultant is that he is less disturbed by the many uncertainties and intangible aspects of OD work. He is not disabled by them but acknowledges that he has to live through such periods. He does not constantly require confirmation from the client of the value of his work. He thinks and works in timescales of years, sometimes decades, and is happy to wait patiently for natural opportunities for interventions to present themselves as opposed to forcing his own pace.

Part of tolerance for ambiguity is concerned with matters of direction, problem definition, personal and organizational aspirations, ambitions, and values. The centred consultant seems more concerned to help others become clear about their aspirations and ambitions, to find their own directions, define their own goals and to think through various routes towards these goals together with the implications and repercussions of various courses of action.

> My strategy is to let things evolve, clarify things, help people focus . . . create an umbrella — which means to carry out an experiment . . . broad direction but no precise strategy . . . help in the true sense as opposed to being directive — to provide an umbrella to warn other managers off, perhaps even the chief executive would be interested. My job is to keep them appropriately informed, so that they feel secure, they know what is happening and are not over concerned about it.

In short the centred consultant here is describing himself as genuinely facilitative and open to the possibility of other people's ambitions, aspirations and values. In contrast we found that some practitioners were in a variety of ways trying to impose their own perceptions, ambitions, and understanding onto others, as if at times their objective was to persuade the client to buy their definition of the situation. In some cases they were fully aware of what they were doing and had reconciled the discrepancy between such an approach and the more typically neutral facilitative stance as in the following examples:

> I've seen participation working successfully in some companies whereas those people at the client organization have not. This in a way gives me some kind of justification for being prescriptive, the expert role if you like.

> One can either say the non-evaluative thing and say well if there's no felt need now for participation we won't give you participation, and leave it at that in which in most cases I think there's no change because there's no felt need or pressure for participation, or you can say which makes me feel more comfortable now, . . . you know it's worthwhile giving it a try, that I'm going to be prescriptive and I'm really going to sell you this one.

Others seemed less aware of the inconsistency between their espoused values of helping the client as a neutral facilitator and their actions which seemed to ensure dependency by the client on the consultant and which also implicitly expressed a distinctive normative stance (See Chapter 3).

The following statements portray a style of consulting where the consultant seems to be trying to retain a high degree of control over events; what the problems are, when they will be handled, by whom and how; approaches which seem as if the consultant is working hard to get the client into a position that the *consultant* feels happy with.

> At the moment I'm holding back on everything except the authority issue which I'm trying to bring out into the open but in as gentle a way as I can.

> I make sure that in diagnosis they cover all of these things. I don't actually tell them this but I make sure that they do.

> He declared his interpersonal issues within the group, one or two of the others wanted to declare theirs, and we said 'no, not now', because it was right at the end of the meeting, but 'hang on to that let's have a session of three or four days when we'll really fragment the thing then we'll build it all together again'. We felt that *we would never be able to contain it at that stage*, we felt that they would go away from that meeting dejected, depressed, and fragmented. Ideally we would have said 'well to hell with the time span', but we couldn't because of the bureaucracy of the place. (Our emphasis)

> If I can get enough of the group to say 'we want to do this' because then it becomes their agenda and they do it, and I'm only there . . . hopefully at the end of it they say we didn't need that guy either anyway. That would be super.

We believe that each of the above statements reveals attempts by consultants to retain control over events by manipulating people to say or do things in accordance with the consultant's wishes. Related to these activities was a tendency on the part of unintegrated consultants to anticipate events with keenly developed yet rigid images of what would take place, who would do what, and what would be the general sequence of events, usually seeing the consultant as key to the activities. Such an attitude is the opposite of pragmatic or contingent. Such people placed heavy emphasis on planned or staged events, and seemed extremely reluctant to exploit natural opportunities when they arose, preferring to defer a discussion or a confrontation until everything could be pre-planned, arranged. It is as if the unintegrated practitioner is attempting to resolve his inner turmoils by manipulating his external world. Associated with these attitudes were two related phenomena; a tendency to look towards a Utopian state whereby a forthcoming activity would prove to be a major turning point, and secondly repeatedly being taken aback and badly disappointed when events did not unfold in the direction anticipated. The experience of having been 'let down' by others was common. For some of our interviewees there was a marked cyclical pattern of events (see Figure 1), beginning with the enthusiastic anticipation of an event, perhaps an opinion or attitude survey, perhaps a new MD, or possibly a set-piece meeting off site.

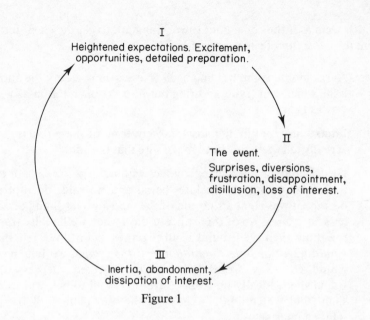

I
Heightened expectations. Excitement,
opportunities, detailed preparation.

II
The event.
Surprises, diversions,
frustration, disappointment,
disillusion, loss of interest.

III
Inertia, abandonment,
dissipation of interest.

Figure 1

The interventionist would describe in elaborate detail his expectations of how events would unfold, who would take which roles, and so on.

This is followed by stage two, the much heralded event, which, almost invariably, did not follow the course that the consultant anticipated (and had planned for), and which left the consultant feeling disappointed, frustrated, and possibly angry and resentful towards those people who 'sabotaged' his event. Sometimes something worthwhile could be salvaged but the most common reaction is that of disappointment. Stage three, the follow up, was marked by little or no action, inertia, a marked lessening of interest by the consultant, and sometimes an abandonment of the project altogether. Finally the cycle is completed by the identification of new opportunities and possibilities, a renewed excitement and a fresh set of plans; a return to stage one.

Stage I Opportunities, Excitement, Plans, and Expectations

Eventually we are going to have two days away. The vehicle is personal objectives, but is secondary to task objectives. There will be two of us, the external and myself. We will take the role of trainer, to try and get them to look at some of the things going on in the group—to try and open it up—to talk to them about the interpersonal problems that they've got, to demonstrate some of the listening skills, some of the skills of managing conflict, intra group skills, are what we are trying to get the group to recognize and then get them to work on these . . . If we can demonstrate in the here and now that something isn't working as it should.

A new MD . . .

> We would try and make some sort of intervention with the new MD if we could get alongside him we might help him to do some diagnosis which would then be a vehicle for him to open up with his management team as something that they might examine.

Getting it right beforehand . . .

> We felt we couldn't go in on an open ended session. We had to go in with something prepared.

> You've got to have complete and utter confidence in each other before you face the client. Whatever difference of opinion we may have we must thrash out before we face the client because we must not confuse the client with our own internal confusion. I don't mind being open with the client, it's not that, I think all we do is clutter up the problem that the client's got or the issue we're trying to resolve with the client.

> We agreed beforehand, now what do you think is the objective of this meeting, and I said, 'in our wildest dreams of course the thing to do would be to get him to accept our diagnosis and to actually have a meeting of the Chief Executive and the Personnel Directors to actually confirm whether or not what we were saying to him was actually true or not', because some of them had said that they would talk in front of that group.

Heightened expectations . . .

> that's very important. This meeting has been set up so long now. Everyone's got tremendous expectations. If something screws it, it's a lot of a let down.

Stage II   The Event

Briefing the actors . . .

> We set up the intergroup session. We gave them a task and we gave them some learning goals which we briefed them about and then we set the thing in motion.

> The MD had agreed that we would meet on the night before and we would actually have a whole day session. And he also agreed with the three or four pages that we'd written for him would be distributed to all the people before the meeting, that he would have

a pre-meeting of an hour or two at which all three of us could be present so that if there were any points of clarification that anybody wanted they would have it there.

As the event unfolds however, things begin to go awry — the actors miss their cues . . .

I was waiting for the other two to come in and say, 'well, what is the real problem?', because we hadn't heard anything for the first hour and a quarter and nothing happened. So in the end I said, 'Well, I may not be hearing you right but I haven't heard what the real problem is yet. Would you like to explain it to me?'

Some of the players find the plot unrealistic and begin to baulk:

One group was very much process oriented. The other group were so task oriented that they didn't link with the other group. They started experimenting with process. On the third task this group thought the whole thing was unreal, superficial, irrelevant, and so on and therefore they tried to inject a bit of aggro into the discussion.

At times key members of the cast refuse their roles altogether and try to interfere with the direction . . .

I thought I was helping him by talking to him after meetings about how the meeting had gone, he replayed it back to me. I used to try and probe him in that way. Let's go back to where we were in the room and let's look at what things were important to you at the time. That was a dreadful mistake because at the next meeting he said, 'well, come on Mr Behavioural Scientist, tell us how to sit around the room'. It gave me all sorts of problems because people started viewing me not as a member of that team but as an outsider who was really looking and commenting and spying and feeding back and so on into all the things that might have been going on in the meeting.

Such acts of sabotage invoke a sharp rebuke;

I went back to him afterwards and asked him how he thought saying that affected me and how it affected the rest of the team. It was a cheap trick, a scoring point. He didn't realize what he had done.

On occasions, despite the abandonment of the original script, the event was considered to be worthwhile after all:

While it didn't go along with the task that we had set them, or it didn't go along with the learning goal that we had hoped would come out from that learning session, it was extremely valuable in terms of getting that group together, it was a good activity.

Stage III   The Follow-up

The most common feature of this stage is that nothing seemed to happen as a result of the event. Projects are either abandoned altogether because of external events, or fall victim to organizational inertia and delays. Things just peter out:

> Quite simply nothing has been happening on the Personnel study despite my asking from time to time what's been going on about it.

> We're way behind plan because one of our main plans of our strategy was to get to the new MD before he arrived in July. Now you know nothing has been done on that. In other words, we agreed the implementation plan. It was fouled up a bit because John Black wasn't at the meeting or left the meeting early and then we thought we had three hours and we only had an hour with him. We could never actually replay that meeting which is what we were going to do to him because he was off sick for weeks so that the detailed strategy of the intervention with the new MD before he came was never worked.

> The next departmental meeting was blown again. It was put off and put off. Originally it should have been four days or five days, eventually it was cut down to two and a half days.

> The thing that messed me up was how important was it to him. I would have liked to have dealt with that out of the meeting. I didn't want to take time out of the meeting to deal with it. I would have liked to have dealt with it but . . . .

> For some reason or another something has screwed up the event on the 5th September meeting. The Production Director had one and a half hours, not three hours as scheduled. He didn't give us a reason and we didn't challenge him on it.

A final, and ironic stage in such a series of events can come with a new set of plans:

> In other words, nothing has happened, but we have set up this series of meeting and if I just run through what the meetings are then I think it will give you some indication of the way we're trying to move over the next month or two.

Plus ça change . . .!

Use of Concepts

By this we refer to several things; the nature of concepts used by intervention-ists, the extent to which these concepts were inherited or had become internalized, the interrelationship of concepts, whether they fitted into a wider framework or organizing theory or whether they constituted an assortment of different and unrelated items. Finally we refer to the internal consistency between an interventionist's account of his actions and the theoretical concepts used to label those actions.

Compared to unintegrated practitioners, centred consultants had evolved more of their own personal concepts to describe what they did and how they understood situations, and employed correspondingly fewer of the more widely used terms to be found in the OD literature. These concepts were often analogic so that, for example, one consultant described his relationship with a client in terms of 'providing an umbrella', 'acting as his tail lights', 'helping him to build a cathedral', 'trying to help him seal up the colander underneath him'. When they do use the OD jargon it is grounded convincingly in their own experiences and can take on a highly personal and idiosyncratic meaning, as in the following example:

> The OD goal at the moment is on the one hand to be opportunist, on the other hand to be consistently checking diagnoses, partic-ularly around readiness and in particular around the readiness of key leaders.

. . . and how do you recognize 'readiness'?

> The non-verbals would change to begin with, the look in their eyes will start changing . . . the amount of time they take over saying that will tell me . . . the speed with which they leave those sorts of statements will tell me that . . . there will be that sort of stuff which will tell me that it's beginning to crack . . . like they're going to say, 'Well we're coming towards the end of a meeting, we've got one in a month's time, but I rather think we ought to get together rather more quickly on this, can you make something like tomorrow?' And then I should normally say, 'Well, what do you want to get together that fast for' and they'll say: 'Well, really, I think we ought to get on with this don't you?' instead of 'We've got a meeting in a month, why not let's swap agendas before we meet . . . which means it's their stuff they're working on, they're in control of the pace the direction of the event, and it isn't something they're trying to get up and do. Those sorts of things will tell me first that they're ready.

Centred consultants have built up their own personal stock of concepts and link them together with theories that have been grounded in experience. Unless they can find the meaning for a concept within their experience, it is rejected and replaced perhaps by a more appropriate creation of their own, often tailoring it to the specific context of the client organization as in the following statement:

> I picked the word innoculate and crystallize, things, words, which are akin to their technological culture . . . In a way it cuts through to them, it bridges the gap between different languages of communication.

They are cautious in their use of labels and concepts and often suggested that their actions were for reasons that they found difficult to define precisely. Sometimes they used the term intuition to explain this and on other occasions they referred to feelings or sensing something:

> When I said that, I said it because *I do all things intuitively*. My post rationalization is that really what we're about in that department is ownership throughout the whole structure. Trying to get an ownership of change, not just this top management box.

> Actually I don't know what my view is (of participation) either. It just *seems* to be worth moving to the next stage.

> Don's phrase about music rather than words, the focus of what we were talking about was on the music of participation rather than just the straightforward formal words of participation; the whole process, the dynamics of it.

> It's not the level of thought that I work at. Perhaps we do it intuitively without worrying about it.

> You have a framework, and I think after working together for a period of time you develop a sense of what the other one, what's passing through the other's mind. Like I sensed that Monday morning that we'd said enough, or now it's time to bring Stephen in, now time for me to stand back, and we tend to sense that.

> You develop a feel . . . a feel for who is genuine and who is moaning.

It is this recognition and acceptance of (perhaps even respect for) the indefinable and intangible basis for some of their actions that is a typical quality of the centred consultant. It is as if they believe that their actions cannot always be satisfactorily captured by applying rational and objective labels to them. On occasions they actively resist applying labels to some aspects of their activities:

The problem was that the chief engineer had had a heart attack and was missing, another man was missing, two of the fellows were new in the last eighteen months. They were faced with thinking they really ought to take time out again and start to look at what needs doing and *by some process that I don't know (I've got some feelings on it but I don't think that they would be helpful to you on the tape because I can't really put a tag to them)* I was invited to a meeting of that group.

In short centred consultants are not captives of OD terminology, they do not reify concepts but use them expediently, cautiously, and supplement them creatively with their own personal and rich imagery.

Unintegrated practitioners are characterized by a greater reliance on what might be termed second-hand concepts and theories derived either from the literature or from other practitioners:

> Consultants have done a lot of work developing 'open-systems' packages so a lot of the stuff that we use has come direct from them. I find this a very helpful way of visualizing organizations.

> I would normally think of organizations as open systems and in analysing them I would use an approach where they look at internal systems in an organization, social systems, task systems, technology. In designing organizational instruments I would cover these areas, and in looking at the environment outside the organization what things impact on it, and then try and decide where an organization is now; where it is going, where does it want to be, how will it get there, and then use a force-field analysis.

We would not wish to deny the usefulness of such theoretical frameworks but rather to point to some of the consequences of becoming dependent on externally generated perspectives, as epitomized and characterized in the unintegrated practitioner. We see the risks mentioned below.

First, there is the risk of becoming trapped by a framework. By this we mean becoming so reliant on one predominant explanatory device that one is blinded to alternative viewpoints and explanations. In its extreme form this entails becoming obsessive about one particular feature of a client's activities and possibly failing to notice and deal with other issues which may be of greater importance. In the following quotation for example the consultant has a preoccupation with boundaries:

> Some of the complication between us is—there's not a clear boundary between them, and there isn't a clear boundary between these two—there's a business development unit and there isn't really a clear boundary between all of them because they are short term and that's long term and where does the line stop?

A second risk, as we see it, is that such frameworks and concepts may draw attention away from those things which centred consultants seem to value and hold significant, namely the unnameable, the intangible, intuitive, sensory aspects of organizational life. Indeed it may be that it is precisely these aspects that infuse meaning into the concepts and theories of OD for centred consultants, but which are inevitably lost in the process of reifying the concept through the written or spoken word. Hence the notion of 'singing other people's songs without even knowing what the songs say'.

Thirdly we found evidence of some practitioners espousing certain values, attitudes and practices concerning how they went about intervening in an organization, seemingly unaware of glaring contradictions in these accounts. We came to describe this phenomenon as conceptual disjunction. By way of illustration, consider the following pairs of statements. Both statements in each pair are made by the same person.

(a)   How does anybody influence anybody? Some people can do it, I'm not saying I'm good at it. *I don't use the power structure.* I don't use that very much because that's frighteningly ineffective usually; to try to get somebody to crack down on somebody, you get these kind of win/lose positions and I don't have to tell you it's hardly part of the OD ethic anyway. I mean you are trying to build on the strengths and the energies that are already there, rather than put pressure on them to accept somebody else's view.

(b)   *You need always to find out who the levers are* and you have to work with them. And then you have to look at the relationship between those levers and the people in power in the other inter-dependent systems that you're worrying about . . . Levers . . . *people who are powerful*, and I'm referring here to the *real and unofficial*, if you like, the *power structure*.

(a)   From where I sit I believe that the key issue is that we've not got the right climate even in our own management meetings. What are the symptoms that would make me think that the climate is not right? It might be, for example, that we're not sufficiently *open in discussions*. We tend not to say precisely enough what we think.

(b)   The thing that screwed me up was how important is it to him. I would have liked to have dealt with that out of the meeting. *I didn't want to take time out of the meeting to deal with it.* I would have liked to have dealt with it outside but . . .

(a)   My job is that of *continuity*, that of *catalyst* and that of putting things down on paper afterwards.

(b)   *I make sure* that in their diagnosis they cover all of those things. *I don't actually tell them this* but I make sure that they do.

We have considered various explanations for this phenomenon. It may indicate that such poeple have never been fully honest with themselves about what they are really doing, or that they are simply unaware of the discrepancy between their actions and the labels that they apply to them. More simply perhaps they may have become habituated to the use of OD jargon and can recite it without having seriously thought about what they are saying. Yet another possibility that we considered is that it may have been a consequence of the process of presenting a professional 'front' to the researchers, which was gradually removed as the interviewee moved away from grandiose generalizations about his work and began describing specific examples. There may be other explanations that occur to the reader. We are *not* saying however that centred consultants are not characterized by such contradictions but rather that they are more *aware* of them and seem to have the capacity both to learn from them and to accept them. It is the apparent lack of awareness of such contradictions that typifies unintegrated practitioners. This had various consequences as far as we could see. It constituted a major handicap to learning and so resulted in unintegrated practitioners repeating the same mistakes over and over again. It also seemed, not surprisingly, that such people were less fulfilled and satisfied in their work and also their careers, and spent more time looking for stimulation outside their jobs. They described themselves typically as feeling frustrated, unhappy, disenchanted with work and organizations. Some were actively exploring the possibility of changing career. The next section examines some of these ideas more closely.

Self-assurance or Acceptance

This heading refers to the extent to which our subjects had apparently come to terms with their weaknesses and vulnerabilities as well as learning to make the most of their strengths and talents. It refers to their ability to accept the reality of themselves and their roles as agents to change 'warts and all' and to operate within such constraints. To some extent it refers to their skills of self management.

In terms of our definition, those consultants closer to the centred pole of our continuum had a relatively high level of self-awareness and self-acceptance. They recognized their talents and abilities together with their weaknesses and shortcomings and tailored their activities in order to make the best use of themselves.

> I have to, despite myself, to be very rigorous and detailed because I am not. I am a skimmer, an entrepreneur as well . . . another repercussion is that I have to structure and manage time very carefully because I'm also a director of four companies.

> My reading isn't the original research papers, my reading is not what I would call the erudite paper. My reading is very much in

areas where people are commenting on trends, because you haven't got time to do it all and that's the easiest way to do it.

They recognize themselves as being a party to events and seem to accept the political nature of their role:

> The external outside disinterested onlooker, if they've got personality and who are accepted will always be more influential than someone within the organization because I'm a threat to someone else. I'm developing ideas which are a threat to their status, their position, their authority, their responsibilities. You see, this is a fact of life. If you don't see it as a fact of life then you're just putting your head in the sand.

> If something's going to be done differently, it's a consequence of your involvement either because you're standing on your head in a corner or because you're active, you are a party to that situation.

In this respect they were far less naive than many criticisms made of the OD literature would justify.

Finally, centred consultants describe themselves as gaining both fulfilment and satisfaction from their work: some even talked in terms of self-actualization:

> It feels like fun and it feels like self-actualizing, like a pretty reasonable autonomy, although it can't sound like it. I mean it ought to be but it doesn't feel like 'Oh Christ, I'll do another day's consulting' and so on.

Centred consultants, then, have evolved their own distinctive approach to their work. They have acquired or created ideas and theories which not only accord with their experiences but help them in terms of both understanding situations better and acting more appropriately in them. They acknowledge the difference between their roles and approaches and those of other people without feeling the need to justify or defend their position. They accept these differences without anxiety and self doubt.

Such self-assurance and acceptance of differences in others is less apparent in consultants whom we would regard as closer to the unintegrated end of our continuum. Encounters with clients are described in terms which imply a competition or struggle for control, an acute awareness of the 'image' presented to the client by the consultant and a fear of being 'taken over' by the client organization.

> In a way, when you go out you are like going into the swamps, as the Americans call it. You do feel like you've gone out into the

swamps and it would be very easy to be taken over . . . by the organization because in a way you can be more effective if you're slightly eccentric, that it's part of this 'create a disturbance' bit, ripples, not bloody waves which knock everybody over or just screw them to the wall . . . just kind of gentle ripples which makes the boat rock a bit, like they can spot you in the canteen because you've got this bright tie on. Your hair is just a little bit too long. I think you do it so you've got a tag back to your organization, but also you probably feel more effective in that kind of situation and that kind of person.

I get that everywhere I go. I put a tie on for clients and I feel a pressure to dress in not exactly their manner but to have certain of the symbols like a tie, is what is expected. I wouldn't go down to client A without a tie on, but I wouldn't wear a suit to client B or C, that to me would be going too much into their world. What I would tend to do is wear a blue jacket and blue trousers, but not a suit and a rather too bright tie than they would probably expect.

Keeping the client in his place . . .

I sort of chastised him a bit about openness and it's not that common in client A . . . it could just be my manner but I always feel it's a way of pulling him up that I feel I've got a solid enough base to do that. That he knows I'm not saying 'You're hopeless, Jim Brown', just that 'Watch it, Jim, you haven't taken me over completely' and 'I'm still keeping my eye on you and commenting on it'

If I'm right, most of what people need is somebody pressing on their conscience.

Requiring reassurance from the client of the usefulness of an event suggests to us another aspect of uncertainty:

I asked him at the end, 'Did you find this meeting useful?' and he said 'Very useful, because one does become complacent about one's own list' and he said he'd like to make it a regular thing and could you become involved in this and this issue? and so I said 'Yes, happy to'.

Centredness, in this section, implies self-acceptance and self-management; an apparent inner calmness and strength; relaxedness and self confidence that comes from working within one's abilities. It is such qualities that in part may account for the tag 'Guru' that is sometimes applied to such people.

In contrast unintegrated qualities are characterized by uncertainty, anxieties related to competence, image, and strength to resist the tensions and pressures from client organizations, a fear of being 'taken over'.

Conclusions

We believe that our findings contain several implications which are relevant to the future of OD. If we use as a point of reference those people who are apparently in our subjective estimation, the more successful practitioners of OD, the most common characteristic of them would seem to be that of diversity — diversity in terms of style, ideas, theories, terminology. They operate in differing yet characteristic ways.

In contrast to what we have termed unintegrated consultants, their attitude towards and use of theories of organizational change would seem to be that such theories offer a series of starting points or heuristics and that those theories are moulded, amended, rejected in part or in whole, or perhaps incorporated into the consultant's body of theories depending on the extent to which they are found to be useful for understanding and acting in encounters with clients. In short they use such theories very selectively and judge their utility against their often extensive consulting experience. Centred consultants often create their own theories for operating and intervening. These may constitute the eclectic melding of a variety of theories, but often they contain a characteristic hallmark of the individual. Their terms and concepts are not borrowed so much from the conventional terminology of OD as from a more personal and idiosyncratic set of terms derived from their experiences, metaphors being a common source of such concepts.

In short, it appeared to us in general that interventionists who seemed to be effecting more changes had evolved their own range of concepts, ideas, and terminology (which for the most part did not incorporate much conventional OD language); whereas those interventionists who relied more heavily on OD terms (and fashionable philosophies) seemed to accomplish fewer changes and appeared to experience some stress, self doubt and general uncertainty about their role because of the contradictions arising from the language and from using a mixture of other people's ideas.

Unintegrated consultants use theory in a different way, as if it represented a blueprint or ultimate truth towards which they can aspire. They are less able to incorporate discrepancies (between events as they happen and events as they ought to happen according to the theory) into a modification of theory, seeming instead to attribute such discrepancies to bad ritual, or a misapplication of the theory. The unintegrated consultant reifies theory and becomes its slave, the centred consultant manipulates and exploits theory until it becomes his servant.

We believe that centred consultants are more enlightened in their use of theory and that the difficulties encountered by unintegrated consultants are partly a consequence of the unitaristic and prescriptive stances taken by early OD writers and partly as a consequence of the fact that much of the writing was about espoused theory and not about practice theories.

We mean by 'unitaristic' writing that it was built around a set of values and a model of the change process that is now regarded as both simplistic and naïve, in that it implied a one best way to go about facilitating change.

We believe, as we have stated elsewhere, that the processes of human behaviour in organizations are extremely complex and cannot be changed by straightforward applications of simple formulae, nor can they be adequately encompassed by any one theory of human behaviour. Rather we consider that our understanding is still in its relatively early stages and that we not only need to recognize the rudimentary and sometimes crude nature of our theories and ideas regarding organizational change, but that we also need to be constantly in the process of developing new ideas and amending old ones. What is required is a wide variety of different theories about order and change in human behaviour in order that the interventionist is able to choose from among a range of theories that which is the most appropriate. Appropriate in two senses; in terms of the *situation*, but also suiting the consultant, his skills, abilities, values, and personality.

In some respects it is possible to regard centred consultants as mavericks since they often disregard aspects of more conventional OD wisdom and pursue their own directions in their own particular and often charismatic way. In other respects, however, they might be regarded as pioneers who are self-sufficiently exploring new territories, surviving by dint of a combination of their wits, their intuition, and luck. Much can be learned from such individuals, but it requires a determined effort to capture their wisdom and translate it into a more readily available form for others. It may also be the case that important techniques or ideas are being developed and used by consultants which are not at present capable of being communicated because there are no concepts available to describe them. Furthermore it is possible that people's actions and ideas are being influenced and limited by such language and concepts as are actually available. The main significance for OD of such people is that the business of facilitating change can take many forms and need not conform to a single blueprint or dogma. Perhaps some of the most important requirements for success as an interventionist are to develop an approach which is internally consistent in that it is based on theories which have been personally validated in the consultant's experience, and is congruent with his values, skills, abilities, and personality.

References

Castaneda, C. (1970). *The Teachings of Don Juan*, Penguin, London.
Kopp, S. (1974). *If You Meet the Buddha on the Road, Kill Him!* London: Sheldon Press.

Chapter 8

Conclusion
Emerging Themes . . .

It is sometimes the custom to conclude a piece such as this by arguing self-effacingly that the work represents a beginning, not an ending, with an acknowledgement of its inherent weaknesses, an assertion that there remain far more questions than answers and a statement that much more work is required before we can allow ourselves to think in terms of solving the many puzzles presented.

Our decision to not follow this particular convention is because we consider it to be inappropriate to the model of knowledge that we are using throughout this book. We do not view knowledge as a fixed objective 'thing out there' with which we can become increasingly familiar. We view it rather as a process which is neither objective, nor fixed. For us, knowledge is personal, subjective, and evolving.

The ideas that we have presented and discussed in this book should be seen in this context therefore. They do not signify a beginning, a middle or an ending but a reflection, and we hope an integral part, of a continuously evolving process of sense making, of comprehending.

The cycle of fashion is such that not only has OD ceased to be fashionable but the current fashion seems to require increasingly emphatic and colourful assertions of its demise. It is as if some people are competing to find better ways of denouncing OD. Such activities strike us as a spectacular waste of energy, short-sighted, and rooted in a view of knowledge that corresponds to unintegrated practice, namely that somewhere sometime we will find an answer and that we are disappointed and disillusioned to discover that OD has not come up with the goods. Others within the OD community are suggesting that what is presently occurring is part of a dialectical process, that if early OD writing and ideas represent the thesis, and current disaffection the antithesis, that we should look for the emergence of a creative synthesis. Our research is consistent with the dialectical notion that the seeds of a future system of beliefs are to be found within the existing system.

We would suggest that there are signs among some of those we interviewed that the practice of OD is becoming perhaps more mature in three senses. It is becoming mature in the psychotherapeutic sense of an acceptance of, and a coming to terms with, the undesirable and unpleasant aspects of the activity.

Mature also in the sense of accepting responsibility for self as actor and as an agent that is a party to events. Thirdly, mature in being relatively self-reliant, working more from an internal locus control, as compared with a predominantly external dependence on others for answers, techniques, and ideas.

While there is evidence of people still basing their activities or ambitions on some of the early models and ideas of OD we believe that our research indicates that some practitioners have moved away from the early OD model in several significant respects. Among those people there has been a letting-go of some of the early ideas and ambitions and there are signs of the emergence of other emphases. In the following section we highlight eight points which appear to us to epitomize the evolution of OD practice.

Shifting Emphases

From External Authority to Internal Authority

Not many practitioners operate regardless of the ideas, opinions, and advice of others but there would seem to be a body of practitioners for whom such information is of secondary importance to their own relatively robust and characteristic world view. For these people the primary authority is themselves, their own ideas, theories, and approaches. They use other data to modify and supplement their own view but never to supplant it. They seem to be comfortable about rejecting or accepting others' ideas because of the strength of their own viewpoint. For them, far less emphasis seems to be placed on becoming familiar with someone else's theory, or acquiring a technique developed by others, and more on developing their own personal stock of theories and techniques. In this sense they find it easier to remain independent of the various gurus in the field while able to acknowledge their influence. They might be conceived of as a mature second generation of OD practitioners, operating with less of a crusading zeal than the first generation.

From Ambitious to Modest Aspirations

Two trends suggest a dilution of the grandiose ambitions of the original writers. The first is that whereas some still speak in terms of organization-wide plans and programmes, others emphasize the modesty of their ambition, sometimes spending years working with small groups of individuals or a department, or perhaps doing small, piecemeal, projects here and there but with little continuity between them or overall sense of grand strategy. The second trend is the apparently widespread attitude that, for the most part, OD is a very slow, painstaking, and frustrating process that is characterized by frequent setbacks requiring great patience and tolerance for ambiguity. Some of those who retained an image of their activities as contributing to an organization-wide programme emphasized that they considered themselves unlikely to witness the culmination of their efforts on the scale of the entire organization, a career is too short. Organization-wide change is a task to be continued by generation after generation of OD specialists.

From Discrete Finite Projects to Continuous and Seamless Activities

Early OD writing portrays the interventionist as someone who, in response to a felt need by a client, skilfully negotiates entry into the client system, establishes a contract, works with the client to generate data about an aspect of their activities and helps them work towards ways of resolving or living more comfortably with the issues generated before negotiating his withdrawal. Our research has suggested that some people do things differently in several respects.

Interventionists begin working in organizations for many reasons other than felt need. The process of working towards a diagnosis of 'the issue' seems to owe much to the predisposition of the consultant, to his style of operating, and to his preference for some types of problem combined perhaps, with an equally strong aversion to other formulations. Agreeing about a 'problem area' or an issue to be addressed marks a stage in a sometimes complex process of negotiation between client and consultant, and this can be a cyclical process that is repeated many times. Our evidence indicates that 'problems' are not objective 'things' but are defined while reconciling a variety of viewpoints, pressures, and constraints of both a practical and political nature. Set against this picture the doctor–patient model of intervention based on finding out where it hurts and then addressing that directly, seems to oversimplify much of what was described to us.

While the stages of negotiating entry and contracting between a client and consultant were evident, we would wish to suggest, from our work, that this process can be preceded and accompanied by a lengthy period of 'flirtation' between the two parties. This activity may perform a similar function in OD terms as it does in its original context; namely, sensing out potential compatibility between partners in terms of a number of items. Indeed it could give information which is crucial to the success or failure of the entire relatonship.

The 'problem' or 'issue oriented' view of OD fits with a picture of the consultant as someone who becomes involved in a 'project' and is further supported by the discussions about 'withdrawal' which both convey the implication of completing a piece of work. It became clear to us early in the research that many of those to whom we spoke did not share this view of their work. Instead they portrayed their activities as being more continuous, preferring to use the analogy of a stream. The consultant may not be so much someone who helps organizations to solve problems, as someone who helps people transform problems into forms that they or he consider to be more manageable. This interpretation is also consistent with the notion of Watzlawick *et al.* (1974) that the solution is the problem, that absolute solutions, like objective problems, are rare and elusive creatures. Our attempts to solve a problem, or perhaps more neutrally, address an issue, are likely in themselves to create further repercussions which also require some form of action, and so on.

From Evangelism to Pragmatism

One of the most persistent and wounding criticisms of OD has been that it is based on a set of unrealistic values about how people in organizations ought to act, and that it fails to accept the less cosy reality of how they do act. Moreover the strongly humanistic stance of many OD practitioners has meant that some of them have acted as evangelists, preaching the gospel of openness, authenticity, and trust, and indeed, attempting to model such values in their behaviour at work and in their relations with clients. As the social, political and economic climates have changed during the seventies such attitudes made their holders an increasingly broad target for those with a more cynical view of organizations.

This research indicates that the committed holders of such humanistic stances have found alternative, extra-organizational forums or communities in which to express and practice their values and life styles. Many practitioners seem to have substituted their early idealism for a much more hard-nosed pragmatism. Such people not only appear to accept the political realities of organizational life, but acknowledge themselves to be part of it and are explicit about their utilization of political processes to achieve their objectives. As organizational goals have shifted from concerns about the quality of working life, to preoccupations with survival and managing a contracting organization, so the attentions of OD practitioners have been drawn to the harsher realities of organizations' operations. One way of explaining the current emphasis among OD practitioners is that while they may retain humanistic ideals and values (and not all of them claim to), they become more contingent in their approach to accomplishing their goals. The practice of some practitioners has become political.

From Passive Neutrality to Active Partiality

Few of our interviewees claimed that they were mere facilitators who helped necessary change to happen. Many openly declared that they were a significant actor influencing events, even if it was by just being present. Of those who claimed the role of neutral facilitator, invariably their description of their involvement with a client suggested differently. For some the OD role offered an opportunity to experiment with ideas or techniques while some others sought opportunities for research into various aspects of organizational operations. On occasions we were told of the personal (and covert) missions that practitioners were pursuing inside organizations, whereas at other times we found ourselves wondering whether some people were manipulating their clients in such a way as to fulfil their own fantasies of an ideal client organization.

From Planned Change to Plannable Change

Perhaps because of the ambiguity of the phrase and the emphasis that it was given early in the OD movement, the notion of planned change came to imply, and encouraged people to think in terms of, grandiose blueprints for an organization-wide set of activities together with staged sequences of phased activities held together by a master plan. Such an interpretation carried with it the implication of an orderly movement from one phase to the next towards an ultimate state of general effectiveness and an appropriate organization for the circumstances.

This interpretation of the notion of planned change seems to have been superseded by a different view, on the part of some practitioners. This view seems to de-emphasize ambitious and large scale plans or blueprints, favouring rather a concentration on the immediate process of constantly and persistently addressing the issues as they arise. Many of those interventionists we spoke to suggested that they were unsure of how things would turn out but claimed that this was not especially disturbing for them since the priority was to ensure that a client system was actively managing its internal processes, while remaining aware of developments in those key areas that were likely to affect them. The current emphasis is akin to the activities of early explorers who had a vague notion of their destination, based perhaps on rumours and stories of new territories across the water, but, with only very rudimentary maps, needing to draw on all their skills of seamanship to ensure their survival, whilst having to pioneer their own routes. Whereas earlier OD writers and practitioners seemed to emphasize the destination, current practice seems more concerned with good seamanship and keeping the craft buoyant, and with picking a course between the many hazards.

Such a shift of emphasis may be in response to the current economic and political climate of uncertainty and retrenchment which has forced many organizations to set aside their more ambitious plans for growth and development in favour of more urgent priorities of survival.

From Rational to Intuitive

OD has never been short of ingenious techniques neither has it lacked people who are willing to offer prescriptions and models for aspiring practitioners. The literature is bristling with sequential models of the change process, analyses of the dynamics of client–consultant interactions and with suggestions for different forms of intervention.

The realization that language is an imperfect medium for expressing and transferring ideas between people is far from new. Among practitioners there is a growing awareness of this, with the consequence that they appear to be more wary of explicit rational accounts, explanations, and descriptions than formerly and increasingly respectful of less rational sounding information. We have noted the caution, amounting to reluctance on the part of some individuals, to explain their thoughts verbally, or to force them into what would amount to an unnaturally reasoned framework. The major inferences that we draw from this are twofold; perhaps we should acknowledge the limitations and perhaps inappropriateness of seeking to present OD via essentially rational statements. Our second and related point is that such a finding has major implications for the ways in which we choose to progress our profession and for the ways in which we develop understanding in newcomers to the field.

From Self Confident Assertive, to Circumspect Caution

Our final observation has to do with the way in which OD is packaged, or presented. According to much of the early publicity that OD received from both sides of the Atlantic, most people could be forgiven for thinking that here at last was a technology that could radically transform the nature of organizational functioning and the quality of working life.

While the OD bubble did not necessarily burst during the last decade, it certainly sprung several major leaks which have seen it become progressively deflated. During this period the attitudes of OD practitioners to their activities seem to have undergone a parallel transformation. The optimism and enthusiasm of practitioners coupled with a near crusading zeal that was so characteristic of the movement ten years ago has almost disappeared. Many appear to have abandoned their affinity with OD altogether, some to concentrate their humanistic activities in somewhat more amenable circumstances and communities, some have reverted to more traditional and institutionalised roles within the personnel, training, and labour relations departments of organizations, while others have retreated into more 'expert' approaches to consultancy. Many internal consultants have branched out into independent consultancy, often with a little encouragement from their employers.

Among those who remain we discern an attitude far different from the early heady days. The ingredients of this new attitude are something approaching a mixture of faith, modesty, caution, pragmatism, and inquiry. The evangelism has subsided and been replaced by a cautious faith that OD ideas and techniques still have a contribution to offer by way of enhancing organizational effectiveness, but there is no longer the suggestion that OD can provide a panacea. The element of caution may be in part a reaction to the avalanche of criticism sustained in recent years while that of inquiry might lead us to expect a continuing evolution of thought and practice in this area.

No doubt the repeated patterns to be found in the history of management theorising will ensure the emergence of a newly acclaimed way of thinking that profits from the mistakes and successes of the OD movement, but which proclaims its own distinctive identity. The King is dead! Long live the King!

References

Watzlawick, P., Weakland, J. and Fisch, R. (1974). *Change: Principles of Problem Formation and Problem Resolution*, New York: Norton.

Index

Ackoff, R., 66, 81, 83
Actors, 1, 15, 16, 18, 45–48, 51, 52, 57, 110
Ad hoc consulting activities, 87, 89–95
Allison, G. T., 44, 55, 59, 60, 81, 83
Altercasting, 49, 51
Analysis of data, 6, 13, 14, 18–20
Anthropomorphic model of man, 10
Argyris, C., 73, 83

Bachrach, P., and Baratz, M. S., 75, 83
Beckhard, R., 85, 96, 100
Beer, S., 5, 8
Bennis, W., 84–86, 90, 96
Blake, R., and Mouton, J. S., 41, 42, 85, 96
Blumer, H., 59, 60
Burke, W. W., 55, 60, 85, 96

Castaneda, C., 97, 120
Catalyst, consultant as, 21, 24, 39, 50, 115
Centred consultants and practitioners, 7, 97–106, 113–119
Change, agent, 5, 7, 24, 39, 43, 44, 51, 95, 96
    management of, 1, 25, 30, 66, 88
    models of, 88, 90, 92, 93, 95, 120
    negotiated, 7
    organizational, 1, 4–7, 12, 15–17, 19–21, 26, 31, 34, 43, 44, 61, 63, 69, 84, 85, 87–89, 92–95, 100, 103, 119, 120
    planned, 4–7, 15, 59, 84–96, 125
Client, 1, 3, 9, 22, 25, 29, 31, 35, 37, 39, 47–53, 57, 58, 61, 63, 65–70, 73, 76–79, 82, 87, 93–95, 99, 106, 107, 109, 113, 114, 117–119, 123, 125
Closed loop consulting activities, 87, 88, 92, 94, 95
Collaborative approach to organizational change, 6
Concepts, 2–7, 10, 11, 16–18, 27, 28, 61, 63, 94, 95, 98, 99, 112–116, 119, 120
    grounded, 6, 18
Conceptual disjunction, 82, 115
Conceptual stimulation, external consultant as, 25, 26
Consultant, 1–3, 7, 9, 11, 21–26, 29, 51, 55, 57, 59, 61–99, 102, 105, 107, 108, 112, 114, 116, 120, 123, 125
    centred, 7, 97–106, 113–119
    unintegrated, 7, 97–101, 107, 112, 114, 116, 119
Consultant roles, 7, 21–24, 95
    external, 24–32
    internal, 24, 32–42, 91
Consulting activities, *ad hoc*, 87, 89–95
    closed loop, 87, 88, 92, 94, 95
Cultivator, internal consultant as, 28, 37–39, 41, 91
Cyert, R. M., and March, J. G., 44, 60

Data, analysis, 6, 13, 14, 18–20
    collection, 6, 13–19
Didactic model, 28
Dunn, W. N., and Swierczek, F. W., 11, 20

Effectiveness, organizational, 57, 91, 126
Endogenous research, 8
Eden, C., and Sims, D., 82, 83
Expert, consultant as, 23, 24
External consultant, 24–32

Facilitator, consultant as, 6, 20, 21, 24, 50, 124
Felt need, 6, 82, 88, 106, 123
Fire lighter, external consultant as, 31, 32
Fordyce, J. K., and Weil, R., 21, 22, 42
Friedlander, F., 4, 8, 24
Friendlander, F., and Brown, L. D., 5, 8

Glaser, B. G., 10, 20

130

Glaser, B. G., and Strauss, A. L., 10, 13, 20
Goffman, E., 59, 60
Golembiewski, R., 50, 60
Goodman, P. S., and Pennings, J. M., 57, 60
Goodstein, L. D., and Boyer, R. K., 2, 8
Greiner, L., 31, 42
Grounded, concepts, 6, 18
  research, 10, 18
  theory, 11, 13
Guru, 98, 102, 118, 122
  external consultant, 30, 31

Harré, R., and Secord, P. F., 10, 20
Health, organizational, 57
Hewitt, J. P., and Hall, P. M., 81, 83

Impression management, 48, 49
Independence of client, 22, 23, 124
Internal consultant, 24, 32–42, 91
Intervention, 1–3, 5, 6, 9, 10, 12, 15, 17, 23, 26, 27, 29, 35, 39, 45, 46, 48, 58, 61–68, 71–82, 84, 87, 90, 93, 94, 98, 111, 123, 125
Interventionist, 4, 6, 12, 13, 19, 21, 23, 33, 38, 44, 46, 47, 50–55, 59, 61, 68, 70, 85–95, 103, 108, 112, 119, 120, 123, 125
Interviews, 13–18, 20
Issues, 61–82, 123, 124
  construction of, 68–75
  reconstruction of, 68–70
  surrogate, 79–81

Jones, S., Eden, C., and Sims, D., 81, 83

Kahn, R. L., 6, 8, 86, 96
Kelman, H. C., 59
Kepner, C. H., and Tregoe, B. B., 81, 83
Kopp, S., 98, 120
Kuhn, J. S., 26, 42

Language, 4, 15, 17, 63, 64, 74, 113, 120, 125
  organization development, 29, 63, 93, 119
Lewinian force field analysis, 28, 114
Loner, internal consultant as, 40, 41
Lukes, S., 28, 42

McCall, G. J., and Simmons, J. L., 53, 60
McLean, A. J., 7, 87, 96
McLean, A. J., Hyder, S., Mangham, I. L.,

Sims, D., and Tuffield, D., 1, 8
Management of change, 1, 25, 30, 66, 88
Management of impressions, 58, 49
Mangham, I. L., 7, 53, 55, 57, 59, 60, 65
Manipulation, 44, 45, 58, 59, 107, 124
Maruyama, M., 9, 20
Merton, R. K., 66, 83
Methodological, criteria, 9–12
  questions arising, 14–18
Methodology, 1, 9, 20
Micropolitics of organizational change, 36, 43–60
Models, of change process, 25, 85–88, 90, 92–95, 120, 125
  didactic, 28
  of man, 10
  of organization development, 7, 122
  truth/love, 6, 45, 55

Negotiated changes, 7
Negotiated order, 44, 54, 55, 59

Order, negotiated, 44, 54, 55, 59
Organization development, 1, 3–10, 22, 29, 32, 35, 39–44, 56, 59, 76, 78, 82, 84–86, 90–97, 100, 104, 105, 115, 119–126
  centred practitioners of, 7, 97–106, 113–119
  community, 2, 121
  expert, 42
  jargon, 112, 116
  knowledge, 95
  language, 29, 63, 93, 119
  literature, 1, 5–7, 15, 20–24, 61, 84–95, 112, 117, 125
  models, 7, 122
  movement, 3, 125, 126
  people, 57
  practice, 4, 122
  principles, 2
  shifting emphasis of, 122–127
  specialists, 123
  strategy, 34
  techniques, 2
  technology, 5
  terminology, 4, 61, 86, 114, 119
  texts, 1, 2, 45
  thinking, 3, 4
  unintegrated practitioners of, 7, 97–101, 107, 112, 114, 116, 119
  values, 7
  writers, 1, 4, 15, 44, 125
  writing, 5, 121, 123

Organizational change, 1, 4–7, 12, 15–17, 19–21, 26, 31, 34, 43, 44, 61, 63, 69, 84, 85, 87–89, 92–95, 100, 103, 119, 120
  collaborative approach to, 6
  micropolitics of, 36, 43–60
  truth/love model of, 6, 45, 55
Organizational effectiveness, 57, 91, 126
Organizational Health, 57

Paradigm, 11, 26–28
Perinbanayagam, R. S., 46, 60
Pettigrew, A., 57
Planned change, 4–7, 15, 59, 84–96, 125
Political, 3, 7, 32, 36, 43–46, 55–59, 71, 74, 75, 90, 123
Politics, 1, 4, 5, 26, 27, 42–45, 55, 57, 62, 74, 86
Pounds, W. F., 81, 83
Power, 1, 3–5, 8, 26–28, 31, 32, 43–45, 55–59, 66, 69, 71, 73, 75, 81, 88, 90, 100, 102, 115
  second order, 28
Practitioners, 11, 15, 17, 19, 20, 41, 82, 84, 86, 88, 90, 99, 122, 124–126
  centred, 7, 97–106, 113–119
  unintegrated, 7, 97–101, 107, 112, 114, 116, 119
Presentation of self, 49, 51
Problems, 62–65, 76, 78, 79, 81, 82, 123, 124
  construction of, 74
  reconstruction of, 68, 70–71
Provider of world views, external consultant as, 26–29

Research interviews, 13–18, 20
Research methodology, 1, 9–20
  criteria, 9–12
Research procedure, 12–14
Rogers, E., 85, 96

Roles, 16, 51, 52, 102, 104, 110
  consultant, 7, 21–42, 91, 95

Script, 51, 52
  situational, 49, 51, 52, 54
Self-presentation, 49, 51
Sims, D., 6, 7, 65, 77, 83
Sims, D., and Jones, S., 82, 83
Situational script, 49, 51, 52, 54
Sounding board and counsellor, external consultant as, 29, 30
Strauss, G., 5, 8
Surrogate issues, 79–81
Systems approach, 28

T-groups, 41
Tactician, internal consultant as, 33–36, 41
Theatrical behaviour, 45–46
Theories, 1, 5–7, 15, 24, 25, 90, 98, 113, 115, 117, 119, 120, 122
  espoused, 21, 86, 98, 120
  in use, 21, 86
  of organizational change, 119
  practice, 120
Thompson, J. D., 56, 60
Trainer, internal consultant as, 41
Transactional analysis, 41
Tuffield, D., 7, 81, 83

Unintegrated consultants and practitioners, 7, 97–101, 107, 112, 114, 116, 119

Values, 1, 7, 15, 57, 59, 93, 106, 120, 124

Watzlawick, P., Weakland, J., and Fisch, R., 123, 127
Weinstein, E. A., 46, 60
Weisbord, M., 86, 96
White, S.E., and Mitchell, T.R., 10, 20